Chicago's Famous Buildings

Chicago's

FIFTH EDITION Famous Buildings

Franz Schulze and Kevin Harrington

The University of Chicago Press Chicago and London

The University of Chicago Press, Chicago 60637
The University of Chicago Press, Ltd., London

© 2003 by The University of Chicago
All rights reserved. Published 2003
Printed in the United States of America

12 11 10 09 08 07 06 05 04 03   1 2 3 4 5
ISBN: 0-226-74064-1 (cloth)
ISBN: 0-226-74066-8 (paper)

Library of Congress Cataloging-in-Publication Data
Chicago's famous buildings.—5th ed. / Franz Schulze and Kevin
Harrington.
      p.   cm.
Includes index.
    ISBN 0-226-74064-1 (cloth : alk. paper)—ISBN 0-226-74066-8
(paper : alk. paper)
    1. Architecture—Illinois—Chicago—Guidebooks. 2. Public buildings—
Illlinois—Chicago—Guidebooks. 3. Chicago (Ill.)—Buildings, structures,
etc.—Guidebooks. I. Schulze, Franz, 1927– II. Harrington, Kevin, 1944–
    NA735.C4 C4 2003
    720'.9773'11—dc21
                                        2003006701

♾ The paper used in this publication meets the minimum requirements of
the American National Standard for Information Sciences—Permanence of
Paper for Printed Library Materials, ANSI Z39.48-1992.

Contents

Preface to the Fifth Edition

One of the distinguishing characteristics of the arts of the contemporary period is a multiplicity of styles and values that appear and recede in quick rhythm, sometimes even reappearing in slightly altered form. That observation applies to the record of architecture in Chicago, a subject rich enough in its own right to have kept this book alive through four editions and more than three decades of publication. In its first edition as well as in this, its fifth edition, it has sought to keep its readership abreast of the most informed understanding of the city's buildings and their context. It has not always agreed today with what it said yesterday, except in one respect, namely, the conviction that Chicago is the site of some of the most important architecture of the last century and a half and the home of a stellar company of individual designers, including Louis H. Sullivan, Daniel Burnham, John Wellborn Root, Frank Lloyd Wright, and Ludwig Mies van der Rohe.

While that claim is shared by all the text's authors and editors, they themselves have changed over the years in both identity and generational disposition. To be sure, we who have put together this edition would like to believe ourselves free of the intellectual bondage of the moment. Yet we are aware that critical objectivity is difficult to sustain, a viewpoint evident from the alterations in the approach to our subject that have marked and enlivened previous editions.

In large part the first edition grew out of the organization in the 1950s of the Commission on Chicago Landmarks. As such, attention was focused on cherished individual buildings (hence the title of the book), particularly those associated with what was commonly known as the Chicago school, a body of technically inventive, formally bold, expressively straightforward work from the late nineteenth and early twentieth centuries that was credited with shaping much of the modern architectural aesthetic. The architects were celebrated not only as exemplary masters but as revolutionaries, whose efforts, Ira Bach wrote in the foreword to the first edition, added up to "the most important innovation in the art of building since the Gothic cathedrals."

It is well to remember that Bach's heady superlative was fully in step with mainstream critical thought of the mid-1960s. The success of the first edition and the acceptance of its point of view were apparent in the publication just four years later, in 1969, of the second edition, which differed from its predecessor only in the extensiveness of its coverage. It made room for a number of new buildings that seemed to constitute a revival of the old Chicago school and for the suburban work of Frank Lloyd Wright and his followers.

In the third edition, in 1980, on the other hand, a significantly modified outlook was discernible. The Chicago school as defined was no longer taken as the prime measure of quality in Chicago building nor was the historic importance of the city's architecture rated so highly or asserted so unconditionally. Historicist as well as modernist buildings were included, and organization followed geographical lines rather than strictly stylistic or technical categories. Not only single buildings but whole areas or neighborhoods were cited, often of various or anonymous, as distinct from individual, authorship. If not explicit, the more broadly accommodating attitude called postmodernism, so influential in international thinking about architecture in the 1970s and 1980s, can now be retrospectively inferred from passages in the third edition.

The fourth edition amplified this viewpoint, combining neighborhoods into whole districts, adding several new comprehensive essays, including more vernacular buildings, extending its scope over a broader exurban landscape, and acknowledging, in a section called "Dead Buildings" (herein retitled "The Ghost City"), that Chicago's vaunted love of architecture has a dark side, an all too frequent willingness to tear down some of the best structures its designers have put up.

Thus to the current, or fifth, edition. In the course of the 1990s, several subtopics earlier regarded marginally or not at all have moved toward the center, warranting more diligent discussion. Today's awareness of the multicultural history of the United States has suggested a more attentive examination of ethnic neighborhoods and of their citizens' contribution to the material look and spiritual vigor of Chicago. Further to this, the commonplace view of several decades ago, that modernism stood for new buildings and new buildings stood for progress, has not only given way to a deeper reverence for the past but elevated the issue of preservation to a position of highest priority in architectural thinking.

That shift is substantial enough to have affected municipal government as surely as it has the activities of developers, designers, builders, and the public. With the turn of the twenty-first century, it is apparent that Chicago's mayoral administration has given major place on its agenda to the preservation and restoration of historic structures and the purposeful reconstitution of whole areas of the city. No clearer sign can be cited of the importance currently attached to the value of a collective patrimony and the need to keep it vitally functioning.

In this fifth edition, the text has also sought to avoid the trap of nostalgia and worship of the status quo. The issue of the widening net of the cityscape, deplored by some as grievously anticommunal exurban sprawl, but treated by others more neutrally, even affirmatively, is explored here and covered, we think, fairly and as fully as space permits—though not at the expense of our personal judgments. Moreover, and rather obviously, new work in and around Chicago continues to be designed and built, enough of it of sufficient merit to call for expanded coverage in this edition.

We have also newly assumed the role of authors, not merely of editors, thus negotiating a change that in another sense distinguishes this from previous editions. All the entries here represent our own writing, although we happily acknowledge our debt to those devoted, well-informed students of Chicago history who made this book possible in the first place. These include the previous editors, Arthur Siegel and Ira Bach, and the contributors to the earlier texts: J. Carson Webster, Carl W. Condit, Wilbert R. Hasbrouck, Hugh Dalziel Duncan, and Roy Forrey. We wish to express our further gratitude for the support of the Graham Foundation for Advanced Studies in the Fine Arts. Special thanks are also due to Carter H. Manny Jr. and Tim Samuelson for their readings of past editions of the text and to Edward Windhorst for his scrupulous examination of this current revised edition.

Lastly, in recognition of the history of this book, we have made a point of retaining its format and title. It is a handbook, meant to be concise rather than encyclopedic, and intended for a place in a pedestrian's tote bag or a motorist's glove compartment, not alone on a library shelf. And it is first and foremost about *buildings*: the essential object and objective of the art, craft, and purpose of architecture.

Introduction

Chicago's buildings have enjoyed international fame for more than a century. The American Institute of Architects recently judged Chicago the city with the finest architecture in the nation. When this guidebook was initiated thirty-eight years ago, the central concern was to provide access to the significant buildings of the first and second Chicago schools of architecture. These schools have been defined as developing a frankly modern architecture, free of subservience to the past, combined with work that expressed the metal frame as a source of order in large commercial buildings and the wooden balloon frame as a source of freedom in suburban houses. Since the 1970s the buildings that make Chicago famous have come to include many neither designed nor influenced by either the Chicago or the Prairie school. The Prairie school is used to designate the work of a loosely related group of architects formed around the ideas and example of Louis H. Sullivan and Frank Lloyd Wright. Attributes of the Prairie school include an emphasis on the horizontal and

planar, and examples can be found most often but not exclusively in suburban settings and residential expressions.

Chicago's buildings continue to excite interest because of a variety of qualities associated with the city. These are not unique to Chicago, but their particular combination here contributes powerfully to the city's sense of place. The extraordinarily open space and light of the site have found expression in its buildings. While the city's open-framed skyscrapers, with their broad sheets of glass, convey images of space and light, buildings constructed along traditional masonry lines suppress their mass, emphasizing instead the thinness of the wall planes and the abundance of glazed surfaces that describe the psychological relationship between open and enclosed spaces.

Chicago buildings have always been notable for their high level of detail, craft, and finish. This derives from the demands of the architects, the pride of the construction workers, and the expectations of the developers. The standards set early on have always attracted exceptional architects. These include H. H. Richardson, Louis H. Sullivan, Dankmar Adler, Frank Lloyd Wright, John Wellborn Root, Daniel Burnham, and Ludwig Mies van der Rohe, as well as Howard Van Doren Shaw, William Holabird, Martin Roche, David Adler, Bertrand Goldberg, Myron Goldsmith, Fazlur Khan, Walter Netsch, Bruce Graham, Harry Weese, Jacques Brownson, Gene Summers, Helmut Jahn, Ralph Johnson, and Thomas Beeby.

In addition, the leading architecture firms that have operated in Chicago over the past century have exercised tremendous control over the quality of their work; thus, Burnham & Root, for example, could produce masterpieces such as the Monadnock, and Skidmore, Owings & Merrill, perhaps the foremost symbol of corporate architecture in the second half of the twentieth century, could produce such a powerful work as the John Hancock Center or such a graceful one as Inland Steel. Finally, architects in Chicago have always been interested in *architecture*, whether here or elsewhere, and so they tend to undertake the most demanding challenges in their work.

However, as great as many of the individual buildings are, the background buildings of Chicago are of exceptionally high quality, too. Architecture is the city's greatest art form, and this has set a standard for all those who practice here.

For a city distinguished by the great height of its buildings, the six feet that divide the continent between the Mississippi and Great Lakes watersheds on the southwest side of Chicago hardly seem to matter. But it is just that ease of crossing the natural boundaries of the continent that attracted first Native Americans and later ambitious immigrants from the rest of the world to the city whose name has been said to mean "swamp," "smelly place," or "wild onion." This site, promising the easy exchange of commodities, culture, and ideas, has been continually reinforced in the two centuries of Chicago's growth—first with waterborne shipping, later with railroads, then with the automobile and truck, and most recently with air traffic. Even power distribution networks—the electrical distribution grid, the natural gas pipeline system—and information systems—telegraph, telephone (copper wire, fiber optic, and wireless communications)—have also reinforced this vast man-made crossroads of Chicago.

Bearing a Native American name and first settled by Jean Baptiste Point du Sable, a trader of African and European heritage, the city has primarily been a place of manufacture, commerce, and trade. The flatness of the site, the pliancy of the river, and the vastness of the lake seemed to receive the mile-square grid of the Northwest Ordinance as an extremely loose fabric into and through which a metropolis could be woven. Since the ordinance was developed to define an agricultural republic, it offered the same neutral form for towns and cities. Lands designated for public purposes—schools and local government—were allocated according to abstract formulas and vague ideas of urban order. Small towns, especially county seats, located their political and commercial interests on and around the courthouse square. But for a great city, the grid was ill equipped to accommodate hierarchy, focus, and large-scale urban order.

Thus, Chicago grew in an amorphous manner, leading visitors to see it as chaotic. From Burnham's 1909 *Plan of Chicago* to the present day, designers have tried to impose order and focus with varying degrees of success. Chicago's stunning natural resource is the lake, with its continuous shoreline of beautiful parks, which exists because the lake has been continually filled to achieve it. The development of coherent areas emerged from the relation, built up over time, of the buildings with one another and the spaces they collectively define and create, rather than derived from either the character of the site or the focus of the urban plan.

Often, along LaSalle Street or Printers Row, for instance, these spaces narrow and help define the street. Occasionally, for example, at the Federal Center or in Daley Plaza, these spaces emerge as the result of redevelopment. In still other circumstances, along the river or in Grant Park, these spaces have developed into happy amenities after first being treated in an offhand and cavalier manner.

At least since the time of George Pullman, the city has witnessed the competition between people of wealth and power who wish to do well for their employees and organizations of those employees who prefer to look after themselves, without the help of paternalistic business owners. After nearly a century of trying to ignore the city's black population, shortly after World War II the white power structure began to address some of their needs, often through new housing. The results were famously mixed. The Prairie Shores and Lake Meadows apartment developments on Chicago's Near South Side and the later Stateway Gardens and Robert Taylor housing complexes illustrate how a similar architectural idea—tall apartment buildings widely separated in an open landscape—could have radically different social consequences. The Chicago Housing Authority is well advanced in the destruction of the overwhelming majority of the high-rise buildings it had constructed for families.

The public institutions—libraries, museums, symphonies, universities—have always benefited from success in the private sector. State and federal government have seen their responsibility to be one of enabling rather than directing private action. Public corruption has occasionally attracted reform, usually as new separate public agencies—park commissions, forest preserves, public building commissions. The public agencies necessary to organize and coordinate the development of the region have never, however, been expected to generate an illuminating "vision." That role has always been assumed by the private sector.

A building must be experienced for itself, in real time, in person. Photographs may give us an idea of a building's appearance, but only a personal visit permits full understanding. If this is true of individual buildings, it is even more the case for the environments identified here. Even the most sophisticated observer of graphic images would find it difficult to identify the great spaces and places of a city reliably. Once in the city, however, one cannot help but appreciate the quality of these places. Images of other cities—the mountain range of Manhattan, the interconnected squares of London, the radial boulevards of Paris, the broadly encompassing ring of Vienna, the fortuitous tightness of Strasbourg, the interconnected imperial and papal order of Rome—are unable to explain Chicago. This is a new urban form, derived less from any generalized concept and more from the individual qualities of its famous buildings.

(Note: Unless otherwise specifically noted, private residences are not open to the public.)

Maps

MAP 1 The Loop

Grand
Illinois
Hubbard
Kinzie

60 Merchandise Mart

61 Reid, Murdoch & Co Bldg

62 Marina City

63 IBM Bldg

6 Seventeenth Church of Christ, Scientist

Wacker

59 333 West Wacker Dr

64 35 E Wacker Dr

Lake

48 James R Thompson Center

Richard J Daley Center

26 Delaware Bldg

18 Page Brothers Bldg

19 Chicago Thea...

58 Morton International Bldg

46 Savings of America Tower

47 City Hall–County Bldg

Randolph

27

20 Marshall Field & Co

14

Washington

28 Brunswick Bldg

21 Reliance Bldg

Union Loop Eleva...

15

57 Citicorp Center

56

55 Civic Opera Bldg

Riverside Plaza

Madison

30 Bank One Bldg

23 Chicago Bldg

22 Carson Pirie Scott & Co

50 AT&T Corporate Center/ USG Bldg

Monroe

29 Inland Steel Bldg

54 Hartford Plaza

45 135 S LaSalle

31 Marquette Bldg

52 St Patrick's Church

51 Union Station

53 Sears Tower

44 Rookery Bldg

Adams

32 Chicago Federal Center **32**

17

43 Bank of America Center

Jackson

34 Monadnock Bldg

35 Fisher Bldg

24 Second Leiter Bldg

49 Brooks Bldg

42 Chicago Board of Trade

Van Buren

33 Campbell US Courthouse Annex

36

25

37

Harold Washingt... Library

Congress

Manhattan Bldg

40 Pontiac Bldg

Old Colony Bldg

Harriso...

Eisenhower Expwy I-290

Harrison

Harrison

Vernon Park

Lexington

41 Dwight Bldg

39 Columbia College Residence Center

Polk

Polk

Taylor

38 Dearborn Street Station

8th

9th

11th

Roosevelt

Roos...

13th

Desplaines
Jefferson
Clinton
Canal
Wacker
Franklin
Wells
LaSalle
Clark
Dearborn
State
Wabash

Wells
Financial
LaSalle
Clark
Federal
Dearborn
Plymouth
Park Terr
State
Wabash

I-90/94
Dan Ryan Expwy

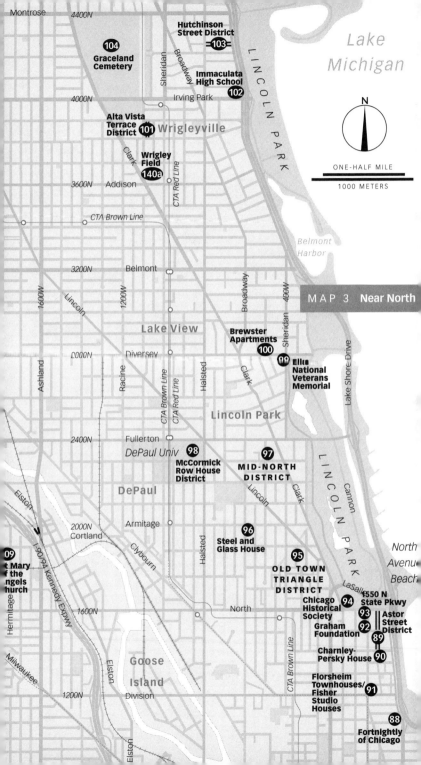

Montrose

4400N

Hutchinson Street District

103

Lake Michigan

104
Graceland Cemetery

Sheridan

Broadway

4000N

Immaculata High School
102

Irving Park

LINCOLN PARK

N

ONE-HALF MILE

1000 METERS

Alta Vista Terrace District **101** **Wrigleyville**

Clark

Wrigley Field
140a

3600N Addison

CTA Red Line

CTA Brown Line

3200N Belmont

Belmont Harbor

1600W

Lincoln

1200W

Lake View

Broadway

400W

Sheridan

3000N Diversey

Brewster Apartments
100

99 **National Veterans Memorial**

Ashland

Racine

Halsted

Clark

CTA Brown Line

CTA Red Line

Lake Shore Drive

Lincoln Park

2400N Fullerton

DePaul Univ **98**
McCormick Row House District

97
MID-NORTH DISTRICT

Lincoln

Clark

LINCOLN PARK

Cannon

North Avenue Beach

DePaul

2000N Armitage
Cortland

Halsted

Clybourn

96
Steel and Glass House

95

OLD TOWN TRIANGLE DISTRICT

09
t Mary
· the
ngels
hurch

Hermitage

I-90/94 Kennedy Expwy

Elston

1600N

North

Chicago Historical Society
94

LaSalle

4550 N State Pkwy

93
92

Astor Street District

Graham Foundation

89

Milwaukee

Goose Island

Elston

1200N Division

CTA Brown Line

Charnley-Persky House
90

Florsheim Townhouses/ Fisher Studio Houses
91

88
Fortnightly of Chicago

MAP 3 **Near North**

Albany Park

Lawrence

4800N

CTA Brown Line

Ravenswood

Lincoln

105
Krause Music Store

Montrose

4400N

Elston

4000W

3600W

Elston

3200W

2800W

2400W

Irving Park

4000N

Grover Cleveland Elementary School

107

California

Western

Irving Park

Central Park

Kedzie

106
Carl Schurz High School

Addison

3600N

Milwaukee

Pulaski

Avondale

M A P 4   **Northwest Side**

Belmont

3200N

Clybourn

I-90/94 Kennedy Expwy

Elston

Diversey

2800N

Logan Square

Logan Blvd

Fullerton

2400N

Kedzie Blvd

Bucktown

Milwaukee

CTA Blue Line

Armitage

2000N

California

N

North

1600N

Humboldt Park

Leavitt

ONE-HALF MILE

1000 METERS

Division

1200N

Holy Trinity Russian Orthodox Cathedral

11

Maps © 2003 by Chicago CartoGraphics

Hermitage

Leavitt

Milwaukee

1600N

North

1200N

Goose
Island

Elston

Division

110 Holy Trinity
Russian Orthodox
Cathedral

Chicago

800N

Chicago

Near West Side

Ogden

Elston

87
Montgomer
Ward & Co

Grand

400N

2400W

2000W

1600W

Ashland

1200W

Racine

800W

Halsted

Western

Damen

Madison

1N/1S

140d
United
Center

Jackson

Ogden

111 Jackson Blvd
District

I-290 Eisenhower Expwy

CTA Blue Line

Harrison

600S

Little

CTA Blue Line

113 Jane Addams
Hull House

112
University
of Illinois
at Chicago

Italy

Tri-Taylor

University
of Illinois
at Chicago

Holy Family
Church/
St Ignatius

114

Roosevelt

1200S

115
Illinois
Regional
Library
for the
Blind

Dan Ryan Expwy

I-90/94

18th

1800S

117 P I L S E N

Schoenhofe
Brewery

11

18th

N

Cermak

2200S

118 St Paul's Church

CTA Orange Line

Archer

Blue Island

ONE-HALF MILE

1000 METERS

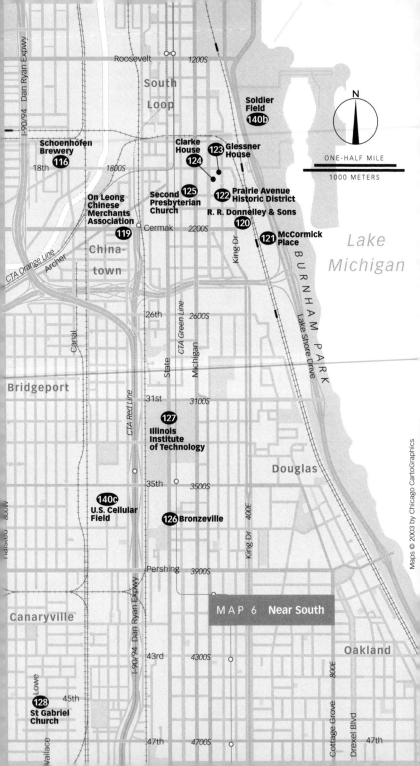

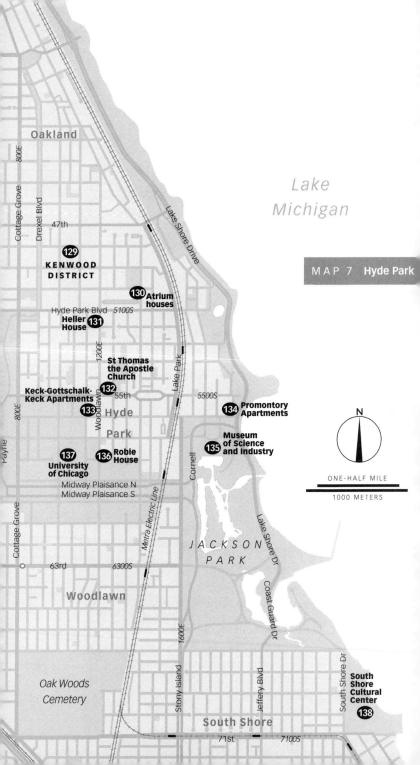

Oakland

Cottage Grove
Drexel Blvd

47th

Lake Shore Drive

Lake
Michigan

MAP 7 Hyde Park

129 KENWOOD DISTRICT

130 Atrium houses

Hyde Park Blvd 5100S

131 Heller House

1200E

St Thomas the Apostle Church

Lake Park

Keck-Gottschalk-Keck Apartments

800E

132

55th 5500S

133 Hyde Park

134 Promontory Apartments

135 Museum of Science and Industry

137 University of Chicago

136 Robie House

Woodlawn

Payne

Cornell

Metra Electric Line

Midway Plaisance N
Midway Plaisance S

N

ONE-HALF MILE
1000 METERS

Cottage Grove

63rd 6300S

Woodlawn

JACKSON PARK

Lake Shore Dr

Coast Guard Dr

1600E

Oak Woods Cemetery

Stony Island

Jeffery Blvd

South Shore Dr

South Shore Cultural Center

138

South Shore

71st 7100S

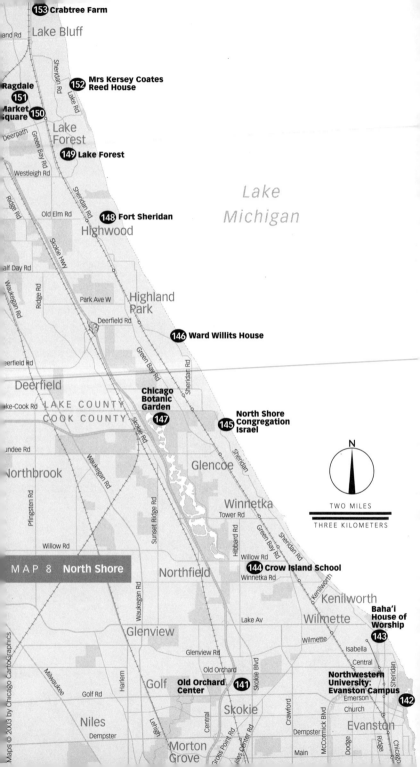

MAP 8 **North Shore**

MAP 9 **Oak Park to Riverside**

RIVER

FOREST

OAK PARK

Frank Lloyd Wright Home and Studio
158

159 **Mrs Thomas H Gale House**

163 **Drummond House/ Roberts House**

157 **Forest Avenue**

156 **Oak Park and River Forest**

160 **Unity Temple**

162 **Winslow House**

161 **Pleasant Home**

FOREST PRESERVE

Madison

Harrison

I-290 Eisenhower Expwy

Columbus Park

FOREST PRESERVE

FOREST

PARK

Roosevelt

FOREST PRESERVE

BERWYN

Cermak

NORTH RIVERSIDE

RIVERSIDE

Riverside
164

165 **Coonley Complex/ Coonley Playhouse**

LYONS

STICKNEY

Pershing

Ogden

N

ONE-HALF MILE
1000 METERS

The Commercial Core

The city of Chicago experienced enormous growth during its first hundred years. From a population of 3,000 in the 1830s, the decade of its incorporation, to 300,000 in the 1870s, the decade when it burned, to 1 million in 1890, to more than 3 million in 1930, Chicago's growth rates were staggering. This influx created immense pressure on the central business area for vast quantities of new construction.

The buildings that resulted from the demand, and that over time have served to reinforce it, emerged from a complex web of forces, including personal ambitions of both clients and architects, technological change, and an absence of powerful existing forms or constraints on new ideas, reinforced by the psychological as much as physical impact of the great fire of 1871. Chicago and other American cities that experienced similar growth following the Civil War were inventing themselves and had few models to emulate. The nearly square blocks of the Loop, served by alleys, were transformed from many small buildings lining the streets to vastly larger buildings covering most if not all of their blocks. The walls of these buildings came to dominate the public space of the city as they defined linear rooms open to the sky. In the absence of a hierarchical sequence, the new spaces of the city developed their individuality only over time and largely through the shared nature of the commerce centered in particular areas. Thus, State Street acquired its character through the concentration of great department stores, while Michigan Avenue developed its imposing cliff overlooking the lake, and the LaSalle Street canyon burgeoned around the commodity and financial markets.

Typical of Chicago's transformation through immigration is that the architects were not likely to be Chicago natives, whether the great figures of the turn of the past century—Burnham, Sullivan, Wright, Root, Atwood—or those of the more recent past, from Mies van der Rohe to Helmut Jahn. As immigrants, they tended to repeat the experience of Sullivan, who declared as soon as he arrived: "This is the place for me." Chicago had the ability to seem unfinished and capable of being reimagined again and again. The slab skyscrapers of the 1890s were succeeded by the square donut high-rises of the 1900s and 1910s to be followed by the stepped-back towers of the 1920s. After the hiatus of the depression and World War II, the clear frames of Mies exerted their power for several decades, to be succeeded most recently by a generation of stone-veneered and tassel-topped towers. Designers were inclined to imagine that they could redesign the city in the process of rebuilding it. Burnham's challenge to make no little plans has done more to fire the imagination of others than to encourage them to implement his ideas.

Chicago benefits from this richness of buildings. The ambition of owners to realize the full value of their investments has established a tradition of high quality in materials, details, and realization that may be found in all classes of the city's large buildings.

The business center of Chicago is undergoing a major expansion and transformation. Such distinct places as the LaSalle Street canyon demonstrate how a developed area can strengthen its identity over time. Michigan Avenue north of the river is becoming the third major retail center of the city, succeeding State Street, which had, in turn, supplanted Lake Street. This shift has meant the decline of State Street as a well-defined place in the urban fabric. The restoration of the Reliance Building and several other projects may help the street achieve anew its former prominence. Whether a place inheres in the city's form or not is often the result of its distinguishing architecture, but in the case of Dearborn Street, "place" is not a feature. From the river to its train station, Dearborn Street enjoys the single greatest concentration of extraordinary buildings in the city; yet it has not become a place, in spite of the three distinguished plazas erected along the street in the last generation.

The Loop continues to expand west as well as east along the main branch of the river, while south of the Loop, the vast railroad yards that once created a wall of high-rises have been transformed by low- and medium-rise residential development. Bertrand Goldberg's projects began a pattern of introducing dwellings downtown, a district formerly notable for having few residents. Loft development is strongest around Printers Row and in the warehouse zone to the west of the Loop. Michigan Avenue has also seen the growth of both residential and office high-rises, often in mixed-use developments.

Although the central business district has expanded in the last generation, it still retains its focus and concentration, thanks to the natural features of the river and lake and to such man-made elements as rail and road. Since the invention of the telegraph, pundits have argued that the concentration of people in central cities will become unnecessary. Nevertheless, the demand for face-to-face contact among people of greatly varying interests and needs remains, and Chicago's Loop continues to provide ease of contact as its core has expanded without beginning to sprawl.

Michigan Avenue Cliff   *(entries 1–9)*

The idea of the cliff of buildings on Michigan Avenue facing Grant Park is so strongly associated with the imagery generated by Daniel Burnham for the 1909 *Plan of Chicago* that it is easy to forget that the idea predates the great fire of 1871. Following the fire, much of the debris was pushed into the lake to create the fill for what has become the park, and much of the open space was converted to commercial use—especially rail yards for the Illinois Central. Despite this conflict between a shared public vision for the park and immediate short-term uses as reflected in the exploitation of the lakefront for rail traffic, architects designed the new buildings along the avenue as if they were in fact facing a large, public open space. The first building on Michigan Avenue to achieve the scale, quality, and character now associated with this view of the park came not from Burnham but from Adler & Sullivan in their magnificent Auditorium Building. The Auditorium and—soon after—its Annex created a great gate around Michigan Avenue and Congress Parkway, the same central axis later defined by Burnham and now secured by Buckingham Fountain and Mestrovic's mounted warriors. Further, as one considers the dates of the buildings along Michigan Avenue, it becomes apparent that many were completed prior to Burnham's plan, reinforcing the conclusion that, with his plan, he was consolidating as much as innovating the development of the city.

As with the other notable ensembles in Chicago, this one is not dominated by any single formal attribute beyond what one sees as an appropriate urban scale. Although memory might suggest uniform height, or color or material, even a cursory glance proves that this unified effect derives more from the great scale—over a mile of frontage—than from other, in this case, minor elements. For most of these buildings, their principal facade faces the park, although these facades are often continued along their side street fronts. Many have their main entrances on the side street to accommodate two distinct purposes, for example, as with the Chicago Cultural Center, originally the Chicago Public Library, where the south entrance once led to the library and the north entry still leads to the rooms and great hall of the Grand Army of the Republic. For others, the importance of shop frontage on Michigan Avenue, as at the Railway Exchange, has pushed the main entry and corresponding orientation of the lobby to the side.

The balance achieved between overall scale and variety of architectural forms does not mean that the individual buildings are polite background pieces. Certain associations are reinforced, such as with the use of classical detail in the Cultural Center and Orchestra Hall. The classical motifs of such commercial structures as the Railway Exchange or McCormick Buildings suggest that some architects wished to continue these associations. However, the Gothic imagery in the University Club and Chicago Athletic Association permits other associations as well. Several buildings terminate in towers, but they do not share a single image. The most eclectic may also be the most sedate—as in the combination of a beehive-shaped blue glass lantern resting on four bison heads, which completes a fine imitation of the Tomb of Mausolus at Halicarnassus at the Britannica Center. What unifies the group most effectively is the continuing shared view of scale that the architects displayed. Whether seen from the park, across the street, or right in front, these buildings present a rich visual experience that offers new detail and delight at every distance.

Congress Plaza Hotel (1893, 1902, 1907)
(Originally the Auditorium Annex)
520 South Michigan Avenue
ARCHITECTS: Clinton J. Warren; Holabird & Roche (1902, 1907)

Clinton Warren designed this building to relate to the Auditorium Hotel across Congress Parkway and constructed it in time for the 1893 World's Columbian Exposition in Chicago. Subsequent additions by Holabird & Roche indicate that there was a great demand for hotels along Michigan Avenue. Warren's facade composition indicates the value he placed on providing a design that paid homage to the Auditorium design of Adler & Sullivan, who served as consultants on the project. Warren's hotel and Adler & Sullivan's Auditorium combined to provide a monumental gateway into Chicago along Congress Parkway. In 1909 Congress Parkway became the central axis of Burnham and Bennett's *Plan of Chicago*. Freed of the need to relate to the Auditorium, Holabird & Roche's work expanded the bays of Warren's design into the dominant motif of their solution. This sequence from variety to simplicity in composition has long served to indicate the idea of progressive design evolution in the Chicago school of architecture.

[*2*] **Auditorium Building** (1889)

430 South Michigan Avenue

ARCHITECTS: Adler & Sullivan

The Auditorium, reflecting the ambition of developers and architects to create the finest performance space in the world and to support it with mixed commercial use, was hailed as a brilliant achievement when it opened, but failed scarcely a decade later.

Ferdinand Peck and his backers wished to guarantee the success of a large theater space with the stabilizing support of the cash flow of the hotel and office building that surrounded it. Dankmar Adler and Louis Sullivan received the coveted commission to design the large and complex building. Adler's special strengths in foundations, spans, and acoustics balanced Sullivan's skills in plan, composition, and ornament. The massive granite base and taut limestone upper walls of the facades exploit the round arched forms associated with the late H. H. Richardson, whose skill in addressing the challenge of designing for a very large building also served as a model for Adler & Sullivan. The surpassing success of the acoustics, the sophisticated organization of the theater, and the rich brilliance of materials, surfaces, and colors in the ornamental program pro-

vided theatergoers and hotel guests alike with an experience that compared favorably to the world's great cultural monuments. In addition to
the theater, other notable spaces are in the former hotel and include the
lobby and stairwell, second-floor loggia, Ganz Hall, and the top-floor library, which occupies the former dining room.

Despite its aesthetic and technical success, the complex as a whole
failed. The theater was too large to succeed as a subscription-driven enterprise. The hotel and office building were unable to supply a sufficient
cash flow, and shortly the standards of first-class hotels changed in ways
to which the building could not be easily adapted. In 1905 the symphony
moved up Michigan Avenue to Orchestra Hall (now Symphony Center [6])
and within a generation the opera moved to the Civic Opera Building (55)
on the west side of the Loop.

The survival, preservation, and restoration of the building are as important to the preservation movement as its original design is to the history of architecture. Since the 1940s, architects associated with the
restoration have included Crombie Taylor; Harry Weese Associates; Skidmore, Owings & Merrill; and the Office of John Vinci.

[**3**] **Fine Arts Building** (1885, 1898)
(Originally the Studebaker Building)
410 South Michigan Avenue
A R C H I T E C T : Solon S. Beman

Beman first designed this building as a multipurpose facility for the South
Bend, Indiana–based Studebaker Company. At the time, Studebaker was
a wagon and carriage maker, but was soon to turn to the manufacture of
automobiles. The first-floor bay windows displayed the company's products in the midst of what quickly became Chicago's cultural center. Burnham & Root completed the Art Institute in 1887, and Adler & Sullivan's
Auditorium opened in 1889. Even so, the city grew so rapidly that the Art
Institute constructed a new building in Grant Park in 1893, and Beman
transformed the Studebaker into the Fine Arts Building in 1898. To do so,
he removed the top, or eighth, story, then added three new stories with
far simpler details than those below. Some have criticized Beman for

overloading the facade, strongly influenced by the example of H. H. Richardson. More tolerant eyes see its kinship to the Rookery, where Burnham & Root used similar motifs. Big and little columns, polished and rusticated stone, all combine for Beman's most exuberant elevation. The office and studio spaces of the building remain largely unchanged since 1898, including a mural cycle on the tenth floor. In 1917 Andrew Rebori inserted a theater at the back of the ground floor.

[**4**] **Chicago Club Building** (1930)

81 East Van Buren Street

ARCHITECTS: Granger & Bollenbacher

While the address reflects the fact that the Chicago Club's main entrance is on Van Buren Street, the building truly fronts Michigan Avenue. The architects took advantage of that prize location, not only in the optimally readable facade, but in relating it compositionally to two important buildings just to the south: the Fine Arts Building (3) and the Auditorium Building (2). In deference to its famous neighbors, the Chicago Club Building displays a happy combination of round arched and rectangular window openings.

The present structure occupies the site of an earlier one by Burnham & Root, built in 1887 as the home of the Art Institute of Chicago. When the Art Institute was relocated to its present building in 1893, the Chicago Club, one of the city's most prestigious private clubs, assumed possession of the building, prior to the completion in 1930 of its own building to the design of Granger & Bollenbacher.

[5] **Railway Exchange Building** (1904)

224 South Michigan Avenue at East Jackson Boulevard

ARCHITECTS: D. H. Burnham & Co.; restoration, Frye, Gillian & Molinaro (1985)

Although many Chicagoans have fond memories of the "All the Way Santa Fe" sign atop this building, its official name reflects the desire of its developers to provide a place where the offices of many railroads could locate. Although the soot created by the coal the railways burned and transported was a major culprit in making city centers dirty, the glazed

light terra-cotta of the facades, combined with the refractive bay windows, offered an image of an ideal city as a place of cleanliness and light. One of the investors was its architect, who later addressed the operations of Chicago's railroads in his 1909 plan. In fact the *Plan of Chicago* was prepared on the building's top floor, behind the round windows at the north end of the Michigan Avenue elevation. The building is a square donut, a typical office form of which Burnham & Root's Rookery is another good example. As when the Rookery was restored, the 1985 restoration of the Railway Exchange by Frye, Gillian & Molinaro opened up the atrium to daylight and placed a second transparent skylight at the top of the building to create a plenum for more efficient air handling and greater tenant comfort.

[**6**] **Symphony Center** (including Orchestra Hall, 1905, 1966, 1997)
220 South Michigan Avenue
A R C H I T E C T S : D. H. Burnham & Co.; remodeling, Harry Weese Associates (1966); reconstruction, Skidmore, Owings & Merrill (1997)

Orchestra Hall, designed by D. H. Burnham & Company and erected in 1905, has served since then as the home of the Chicago Symphony Orchestra with a substantial architectural alteration in 1966 by Harry Weese Associates and a more encompassing reconstitution of the hall and buildings acquired adjacent to it, completed in 1997 by Skidmore, Owings & Merrill. The latter project included major changes to the hall proper, including most notably the deepening of the stage to accommodate a larger orchestra; the addition directly above the players of a lofty steel-and-glass acoustical canopy intended to reflect sound across the stage and into the audience; and the installation of terrace seating behind the orchestra. Less obvious are several other changes of comparable consequence. The shape of the theater has been slightly but unobtrusively narrowed toward the front, and the roof behind a new proscenium arch has been raised thirty-six feet. These measures were also meant primarily to improve the acoustics. Even less apparent, but similarly motivated and for more optimal absorption of sound, are the delicately perforated walls surrounding the stage, indistinguishable from solid walls except on clos-

est inspection. New and mostly larger seats were installed, together with improvements in offstage support spaces and mechanical, lighting, and rigging systems. The hall now accommodates an audience of 2,521.

Palpable changes have been effected in the spaces next to and above the old hall. Significantly, the facade of the former Chapin and Gore Building at 63 East Adams Street, lately taken over by Symphony Center, has been restored, assuring the preservation of the excellent proportions of the 1902 design by Richard Schmidt and the sophisticated brickwork, supervised by Schmidt's assistant and later partner Hugh Garden.

The interior has been almost totally made over in an effort to connect the building with Orchestra Hall. The resultant space now houses the orchestra's Education and Administrative Wing and Artistic Support Wing. The latter contains a music library, rehearsal rooms, a radio and broadcasting studio, dressing rooms for the Chicago Symphony Chorus, the Civic Orchestra (a training group for the Symphony), and visiting ensembles. The largest space in the new addition is Buntrock Hall, a re-

hearsal area big enough to accommodate the whole orchestra, and a versatile smaller hall, meant for audiences of two to three hundred. Orchestra Hall and the new wings are connected most visibly by a sky-lit atrium, called the Rotunda, that doubles as a reception area. A six-story arcade, running along the north edge of Orchestra Hall, links Michigan and Wabash Avenues.

Amenities include Rhapsody, a 250-seat restaurant on the first floor of the Education and Administrative Wing, and an intimate landscaped park facing Wabash Avenue. One of the casualties of the changes to the entire complex was the loss of the legendary Cliff Dwellers Club, earlier located on the eighth and ninth floors atop Orchestra Hall, and eventually obliged to move to newer quarters in the Borg-Warner Building directly to the north. The old space has been turned into a donor's facility, the Club at Symphony Center, and the architects have endeavored to model it in the style of the architect of the old Cliff Dwellers, Howard Van Doren Shaw.

Meanwhile, the historic front of Burnham's Orchestra Hall, one of the sights on Michigan Avenue long recognizable to Chicagoans, has been preserved. The style is neo-Georgian, one of the many manners that Burnham embraced in the wake of the revivalism associated with his role as the director of the 1893 World's Columbian Exposition. The redbrick facade is punctuated by limestone lintels, swag ornaments, and car-touches. The trio of tall second-story round arched windows, topped by characteristically Georgian fanlights, animates the nine-story elevation.

Organized by Theodore Thomas in 1891, the Chicago Symphony Orchestra originally concertized in Adler & Sullivan's Auditorium Theatre (2), but moved to Orchestra Hall in the following decade, performing there for the first time in 1905. The first name of the building, Theodore Thomas Orchestra Hall, is carved in stone over the entrance.

[**7**] **University Club of Chicago** (1909)
76 East Monroe Street
ARCHITECTS: Holabird & Roche

Immediately north of the University Club is the Gage Group, whose facades exemplify the Chicago frame, a form that draws attention to the structure of the building rather than to the historical ornament mounted prominently on earlier exteriors. The device had brought fame to Chicago's commercial architecture during the 1890s and the early twentieth century. Yet by 1910 the firm that designed the Gage Group had invested its composition of the University Club with Gothic detail—pointed arches, crenellations, finials, and the like—that reflected a widespread return in Chicago architecture to reliance on historical allusion.

Equally apparent, however, is the assurance with which the principal architect, Martin Roche, negotiated this later shift of objectives. The application of the Gothic style to the shape of a tall modern building is expertly executed here, and several of the major interior spaces are among the most magisterial in the city. Chief among these are the great Cathedral Hall, based freely on London's fifteenth-century Crosby Hall and magnified by the stained-glass windows of Frederick Clay Bartlett. The murals on the ceiling of the richly paneled Michigan Room are also the work of Bartlett.

[**8**] **Gage Group** (1899–1900, 1902, 1971)
Edson Keith and Theodore Ascher Buildings
24 & 30 South Michigan Avenue
ARCHITECTS: Holabird & Roche; Ascher Building addition, Altman-Saichek Associates (1971)
Gage Building
18 South Michigan Avenue
ARCHITECTS: Holabird & Roche; facade, Louis H. Sullivan; addition, Holabird & Roche (1902)

There is no better example of the famous Chicago frame and Chicago window than in the makeup of the Gage Group. The frame defines itself; it is in effect the bones of the structure, with the skin here consisting of the fully glazed horizontal window, the latter comprising a single large pane flanked by two sash lights. As a form of fenestration, it shows up more in Chicago than any other major city. Moreover, since the Gage

Group fronts Michigan Avenue and faces the broad expanse of Grant Park, it is there most readily taken in, both up close and at a distance. All three buildings of the triad were designed by Holabird & Roche, with Louis Sullivan adding the facade of the northernmost portion, and in the process adding the sort of exuberant decoration for which he himself is renowned. In 1902 Holabird & Roche added four stories atop the original eight. The uppermost floor of the southernmost building was added in 1971 by Altman-Saichek Associates.

[**9**] **Chicago Cultural Center** (1897)
(Originally the Chicago Public Library)
78 East Washington Street
ARCHITECTS: Shepley, Rutan & Coolidge (1897); restoration, Holabird & Root (1977)

Chicago had long needed an adequate central public library when Shepley, Rutan & Coolidge won the commission for this building. As the successor firm of the late H. H. Richardson (whose Glessner House [123] is his only surviving Chicago building), they participated in the 1893 World's

Columbian Exposition. Their Art Institute of Chicago had already shown their skills in large, complex, and symbolic public projects. Sited on a small public square facing east across Michigan Avenue to rail yards, the library gave access at either its north or south end. At Washington Street, to the south, one entered between Ionic columns into a vestibule dominated by a grand stairway of Carrara marble inlaid with mosaics. At the top of these stairs is the present Preston Bradley Hall, crowned by a Tiffany dome. Words and images enliven the surfaces of these spaces, celebrating language, literature, and the book. The many languages of the texts acknowledge the multiethnicity of Chicago's people. One text notes the sweetness of finding, in a foreign land, works in one's mother tongue.

The north entrance on Randolph Street uses the Doric order, associated with the military, to lead into the spaces of the Grand Army of the Republic. The GAR was the association of Union veterans of the Civil War. Its grand staircase leads first to a large room, the GAR Rotunda, dominated by another stained-glass dome, this time by Healy & Millet. Beyond is Memorial Hall, where the campaigns of the war are inscribed. Lincoln and Grant are only the best known of Illinoisans who served the nation at the time.

As Chicago's population rocketed from 1 million in 1890 to more than 3 million in 1930, the library was soon inadequate to the demands placed on it. In 1974 the library began its move to temporary quarters in anticipation of a new central facility, which was completed in 1991. Holabird & Root completed their conversion and restoration of the building in 1977. The open U-shaped court on its west side was enclosed with accessible ramps and other services. Renamed the Chicago Cultural Center, the building has a rich and eclectic mix of uses including galleries; performance, lecture, and film spaces; visitor's and senior citizen's centers; a café; a Museum of Broadcast Communication; and offices for the city's Department of Cultural Affairs.

~~~~~~~~~~~~~

[*10*] **Carbide and Carbon Building** (1929)

230 North Michigan Avenue

ARCHITECTS: Burnham Brothers

The Carbide and Carbon Building achieves its urbane sheen and character through devices both typical and exceptional. Its basic massing—a relatively small tower reaching forty stories atop a more substantial slab-like twenty-three-story base—links it to many of the limestone and terra-cotta Chicago skyscrapers of the 1920s. (The building at 333 North Michigan Avenue [68] is a good nearby example.) Likewise its use of ornamental motifs related to the use or name of the building relates it to other well-known buildings. (The Fisher Building [35] by D. H. Burnham, father of the Burnham Brothers, exploits such a relationship.) Here, Daniel and Hubert Burnham modified the ancient use of plant motifs, fiddlehead ferns among them, in the stylized forms associated with Art Deco. These forms relate to one of the origins of carbon in the decay and geological transformation of carbon-based plants eons ago. A material with ancient origins was thus related to modern technology, as the building's original owner is best known for its Eveready brand of batteries. Bronze, gold terra-cotta, and even gold leaf in the ornament highlight the black granite base and dark green terra-cotta sheathing of the building. The build-

ing is currently being converted to use as a hotel for the Hard Rock Cafe hotel group by Lucien Lagrange Architects. Occupancy is scheduled for 2003.

[*11*] **Aon Center** (1974)
(Originally Amoco Building and Plaza)
200 East Randolph Street
ARCHITECTS: Edward Durell Stone Associates; Perkins & Will

This is the giant building Chicagoans love to hate. For his part, Stone followed Louis Sullivan's idea of the tall office building—that it should be "a proud and soaring thing, rising in sheer exultation . . . from bottom to top

. . . without a single dissenting line." Its relatively open site offers spectacular views of the city and the lake from even the lowest floors. At 1,136 feet, the eighty-story building is a bit taller than the John Hancock Center and much shorter than the Sears Tower. The decline in Stone's reputation, the absence of corner offices, and the replacement of the original Carrara marble cladding with the present granite have all helped generate a rich local folklore about the building. Pollutants, some contributed by internal combustion engines, and other factors had so weakened the thin sheets of marble with which the building had been clad that the owners decided to replace them. In the early 1990s, the project was undertaken and the entire building was reclad with granite from North Carolina.

Set along the northern edge of Grant Park, the entry plaza facing the park contains Harry Bertoia's untitled sounding sculpture of 1975. The sculpture and the office building were constructed for the Standard Oil Company of Indiana (later renamed Amoco). In 1986 Perkins & Will designed and built the northerly plaza entrance to the building. Aon Corporation is now the principal tenant since BP merged with Amoco and removed its headquarters functions from Chicago.

[*12*] **Art Institute of Chicago** (1893)
Michigan Avenue at Adams Street
ARCHITECTS: Shepley, Rutan & Coolidge
Additions:
Gunsaulus Hall (1916), Shepley, Rutan & Coolidge
Hutchinson Wing and McKinlock Court (1924), Coolidge & Hodgson
Goodman Theater (1925), Howard Van Doren Shaw
Ferguson Wing (1958), Holabird, Root & Burgee
Morton Wing (1962), Shaw, Metz & Associates
South Garden (1965), Dan Kiley
East Wing (1976), Skidmore, Owings & Merrill
Stock Exchange arch and Trading Room (1977), Vinci/Kenny
Original building galleries renovated (1987), Skidmore, Owings & Merrill
Main entry and lobby restored (1987), Office of John Vinci
Rice Building (1988), Hammond, Beeby & Babka

North Garden (1991), Hanna/Olin
Fullerton Hall renovated (2001), Weese, Langley, Weese

The Art Institute is the oldest home of the visual arts in Chicago. In 1887 Burnham & Root designed and built the first Art Institute building at the southwest corner of Michigan Avenue and Van Buren Street, inspired by the example of the great Boston architect H. H. Richardson. However, when Richardson's successors, Shepley, Rutan & Coolidge, received the commission for the 1893 building, their classically inspired design signaled a shift in style from the Richardsonian Romanesque of their late master and of Burnham & Root's 1887 Art Institute.

The present building, now called the Allerton Building, opened in December 1893 as an art museum after its initial use as an auxiliary space for the 1893 World's Columbian Exposition. It is the first major Chicago building to take the classical forms and light colors of that fair and put them to use in a permanent building.

McKinlock Court is a pleasant oasis where lunch is served in the open air in summer. The classical arcades of the court make a pleasant foil to the *Fountain of the Tritons* by Carl Milles, placed in 1931. This fountain is repeated, along with much of his other work, at his home and studio in Lidingo, just outside Stockholm. Just to the north of McKinlock

Court is Howard Van Doren Shaw's fine, but currently threatened, Goodman Theater.

The East Wing—containing galleries, an auditorium, dining and meeting spaces, other services, and the School of the Art Institute—is aggressively angular in its demonstration of the geometrically based field theory of its architect, Walter Netsch of Skidmore, Owings & Merrill. The high-ceilinged Trading Room of Adler & Sullivan's Stock Exchange (demolished in 1972) was incorporated in the new construction, and the entry arch of the destroyed masterpiece was reerected in a new garden outside the East Wing. Isamu Noguchi's sculpture fountain designed for the American bicentennial is here as well.

The renovation of the second-floor galleries of the Allerton Building restored the inner circulation corridor, with large top-lit galleries on the perimeter. The ample natural and artificial light in the large galleries is excellent for paintings, while the more intimate scale and carefully controlled artificial light in the corridor permits the exhibition of fragile works on paper related to the larger works in the main galleries.

The relatively small lobby and intensely circulatory stair hall, unlike the vast railway station–like halls and rotundas in some other museums, suggest the highly commercial character of the city: visitors wish to get to the goods quickly, not loiter in the foyer.

Most recently, Weese, Langley, Weese renovated Fullerton Hall to reveal the art glass dome, to develop a sympathetic new color palette, and for accessibility. Genoese architect Renzo Piano has been commissioned to design a major addition. Currently it is proposed to occupy the Art Institute's northeast quadrant—east of the railroad underpass and north of Rubloff Auditorium.

[*13*] Grant Park, including the Museum Campus and Millennium Park

This formally composed parkland, extending from Randolph Street on the north to the Museum Campus on the south, is one of the most impressive passages on a lakefront that has no equal among the shorelines of any of the other major cities of the United States.

The history of Grant Park, virtually as long as that of Chicago itself, began on a proud and prophetic note in the 1830s, when the commissioners of the Illinois & Michigan Canal inscribed on a city map the words "Public Ground—A Common to Remain Forever Open, Clear and Free of any Buildings, or Other Obstruction whatever." Despite numerous efforts to circumvent that intention, it has for the most part been heeded, although its success has also been dependent on the plans and actions of later generations imbued with the same vision.

With the approach of the twentieth century, Lake Park, as it was known in those days, was hardly prepossessing. The ground and the buildings standing upon it were rude, most of them squatters' shacks, and the tracks of the Illinois Central Railroad, which earlier had built a breakwater in exchange for the rights to construct a trestle, ran between Michigan Avenue and the lake. In 1890 local businessman Aaron Montgomery Ward took the case for open land to court, winning a victory that obliged the city to tidy up much of the area and keep it free of any more buildings. An exception was granted to the Art Institute (12), which moved into new quarters on the east side of Michigan Avenue in 1893. Moreover, the railroad retained its original alignments. These circumstances notwithstanding, Ward persisted with several legal actions to forestall further lakefront construction.

By 1903 responsibility for Lake Park had been turned over to the South Park Commission, which appointed the Olmsted Brothers (successors to the office of Frederick Law Olmsted) to design the park, newly named for Ulysses S. Grant. The result was a layout based on French precedents that featured the symmetrical organization of tree-lined lawns appropriately adorned with fountains and sculptures.

In 1909 the famous *Plan of Chicago*, conceived by Daniel Burnham with the assistance of Edward H. Bennett, was published. Its goals for the city as a whole were vast and wide-ranging, and hardly less so those applicable to Grant Park. Burnham proposed an extension of the Olmsteds' formal plan and meant to add peninsulas and islands in the lake. More than a few of his objectives were never achieved, but what one now sees in Grant Park is consistent with much of what he had in mind. By the mid-1920s the railroad tracks had been dropped below grade, Buckingham Fountain had been built, and the museum complex south of Twelfth Street (today's Roosevelt Road) had risen on landfill.

More changes were rung in during the ensuing decades, chief among them the 1955 extension of Congress Parkway through the park; the 1986 rerouting of Lake Shore Drive, which added land to the northeast; the 1998 development of the Museum Campus; and the 1998 proposal of Millennium Park.

Museum Campus

MASTER PLAN ARCHITECTS: Lohan Associates (1986)

Field Museum of Natural History (1921)

Lake Shore Drive and East Roosevelt Road

ARCHITECTS: D. H. Burnham & Co. (1909–12); Graham, Burnham & Co. (1912–17); Graham, Anderson, Probst & White (1917–20); renovation, Harry Weese Associates (1978)

Shedd Aquarium (1929, 1991)

Lake Shore Drive and East Roosevelt Road

ARCHITECTS: Graham, Anderson, Probst & White (1929); Oceanarium, Lohan Associates (1991)

Adler Planetarium (1930, 1973, 1999)

East end of Solidarity Drive

ARCHITECTS: Ernest Grunsfeld Jr. (1930); C. F. Murphy & Associates (1973); Astronomy Museum, Lohan Associates (1999)

Chicago's cultural institutions have traditionally been built close to one another and to the downtown center. In the seven blocks along Michigan

Avenue that separate the Auditorium Building (2) from the Chicago Cultural Center (formerly the Chicago Public Library [9]) are the Fine Arts Building (3), Symphony Center (6), and the Art Institute of Chicago (12).

A second major complex—more dramatically sited and made up of the Field Museum of Natural History, Shedd Aquarium, and Adler Planetarium—is somewhat distant from the first in both space and time, though not by much in either dimension. While each of the buildings in the ensemble was designed independently, together they form an attractive and harmonious cluster at the south end of Monroe Harbor.

If one adds a fourth structure nearby, Soldier Field (140), a sports stadium by Holabird & Roche completed in 1925, the group provides an exceptional architectural experience, although that judgment is compromised by a recent ungainly addition. The prevailingly classical mode of the complex is most apparent in the Ionic order of the Field Museum, the Doric of Shedd Aquarium and the Soldier Field colonnade, and even in the central plan and domical structure of Adler Planetarium, ancient Roman devices that are but little disguised by the Art Deco ornament.

A modernist note more fortunate than that at Soldier Field has been struck in additions to two of the older buildings. The Oceanarium, attached in the early 1990s to Shedd Aquarium, is large enough to accommodate whales, dolphins, seals, sea otters, and penguins. Well conceived and well executed by Lohan Associates, it is sited low enough on the lakeside of the aquarium not to interrupt the silhouette of the older work.

The Astronomy Museum, completed by the same firm in 1999, is a glass-covered abstraction encircling Adler Planetarium and meant to defer to it by keeping a lower profile. That goal is reasonably achieved, but the contrast in styles is more pronounced and less congenial than in the still lower placement of the Oceanarium behind the main aquarium building.

In an effort to make the museum grouping more unified and more inviting, the idea of a Museum Campus was proposed in the late 1980s as part of a world's fair intended for Chicago in 1992. The fair was never realized, but the campus plan proceeded and reached completion in 1998. The northbound lanes of Lake Shore Drive were moved westward so that they now run immediately adjacent to the present southbound lanes. The area thus freed of roadway has been shaped into parkland that binds Shedd Aquarium, the Field Museum, and Adler Planetarium across lawns and pathways.

Thus far the project has been a decided boon to the three institutions and their publics. Rising attendance figures testify to that. The greensward north of the Field Museum has been turned into a series of rectilinear gardens that overlook a gentle cascade of rises and slopes, a pleasant diversion from Chicago's customary flatness. Nothing around the buildings is more impressive than the view of the downtown skyline from the museum's forecourt. New plantings, especially the trees, have gradually relieved an emptiness that marked the uninterrupted green space immediately after the Museum Campus opened. There are entrancing details, like the walls of the pedestrian underpass leading to the west, whose surfaces have been imaginatively sculpted in high relief.

Despite the work and money expended on the enterprise, its success is qualified. Pedestrians are winners, but automobile traffic and parking difficulties remain, because most of the people who find their way to the Museum Campus, and to the Chicago Bears football games, come by car. And so will those whose numbers are likely to increase institutional attendance when the aquarium and museum carry out currently anticipated expansions.

Millennium Park (planned for completion in 2004)
Area bordered by Monroe Street, Michigan Avenue, Randolph Street, and Columbus Drive
MASTER PLAN ARCHITECTS: Skidmore, Owings & Merrill
Music Pavilion
East of Michigan Avenue close to Randolph Street and Columbus Drive
ARCHITECTS: Frank O. Gehry & Associates
Music and Dance Theater Chicago
East of Michigan Avenue adjacent to Randolph Street
ARCHITECTS: Hammond Beeby Rupert Ainge
Shoulder Garden
Monroe Street east of Michigan Avenue close to Columbus Drive
LANDSCAPE ARCHITECTS: Kathryn Gustafson, Piet Oudolf, Robert Israel

Pertinent to Grant Park, the most ambitious plan of the last half-century has been the creation of Millennium Park, the twenty-four-acre parcel of land extending north from Monroe Street to Randolph Street and east from Michigan Avenue to Columbus Drive. When Richard M. Daley announced plans for the park in 1998, the intention was that it would be finished in time to coincide with the year 2000, commonly understood as the beginning of the new millennium. That expectation was altered by a combination of factors, including the addition of eight acres to the original sixteen and the construction of several buildings not anticipated at the outset. A series of cost overruns followed, leading to the necessity of adding private contributions to public funds. The project is now likely to be finished as late as 2004.

Assuming that schedule is maintained, the ground surface of Millennium Park will consist of formal and informal pathways and gardens covering an area formerly made up mostly of railroad tracks. Added to this will be an assortment of structures and related recreational amenities. The fundamental original layout is credited to Skidmore, Owings & Merrill. Bordering Monroe Street at the southeast will be the Shoulder Garden, the product of Seattle landscape architect Kathryn Gustafson, Dutch plant expert Piet Oudolph, and California theater designer Robert Israel. At the corner of Monroe and Michigan, separated from the garden by the Millennium Promenade (a broad path meant for outdoor art fairs and similar shows), will be a fountain by Barcelona artist Jaume Plensa. To the north, the area along Michigan Avenue is given over to a skating rink and, to the east of that, a restaurant. Still farther to the east, the most dramatic element in the park is expected to draw the greatest public attention: the Music Pavilion, a band shell designed by another Californian, Frank O. Gehry. Its stage will be surmounted by a trademark Gehry superstructure of stainless steel ribbons, curling upward and outward, that will be colorfully illuminated at night. Audiences will be seated beneath a 700-foot-long trellislike structure of steel tubes with speakers attached to them, a device intended to provide a better acoustical balance than that of the older, more commonplace speakers mounted on poles. As many as eleven thousand listeners will be accommodated in the Music Pavilion's seating area and contiguous lawn.

Directly to the north, adjacent to Randolph Street, and built mostly below grade will be the 1,500-seat Music and Dance Theater, designed by Chicago architect Thomas Beeby of Hammond Beeby Rupert Ainge to house performances by local arts groups. A pedestrian bridge, also the work of Gehry and notable for its stainless steel and sinuous curvilinearity, will connect the park across Columbus Drive to Daley Bicentennial Plaza (named for the mayor's father) along the lakefront.

In keeping with Chicago's traditional reputation as the setting of an exceptional group of modern outdoor sculptures, Millennium Park will boast a mammoth sixty-six-foot-long, forty-seven-foot-wide, and thirty-foot-high stainless steel abstraction by the Indian artist Anish Kapoor. Tradition, indeed, works to the advantage of old objects as well as new ones. At the northwest corner of the park, a semicircular group of Doric columns, the Peristyle, which was taken down after World War II, has been rebuilt by the Chicago firm of OWP&P. That addition followed the reconstruction of the Park District's north Grant Park parking garage, which made for the expansion of Millennium Park from its original sixteen acres to twenty-four.

Tradition again plays a role in the meaning assigned by the planners to the most striking feature of Millennium Park, the Gehry Music Pavilion. The long-standing view that the parkland east of Michigan Avenue should be kept free of buildings has been officially regarded as honored by the interpretation of the ribbonlike superstructure of the Music Pavilion as sculpture and not architecture.

The expected completion of Millennium Park has been felt at the Art Institute (12), where the location of a planned addition by the Italian architect Renzo Piano has been changed from the museum's south side to its north side, so that it will address the Shoulder Garden across Monroe Street and be connected to it via a Piano-designed footbridge.

[*14*] **Union Loop Elevated** (1897)

CHIEF ENGINEER: John Waddell

Although downtown Chicago has been called the Loop since the cable car days of the 1880s, it is the century-long presence of the Loop Elevated structure that has reinforced the name and kept it current. Parts of the city's far-flung elevated railway system preceded its appearance in the Loop. Aside from the obvious asset of avoiding contact with surface transportation, the Loop Elevated had the effect of bringing a measure of order to the confusion of the city's downtown transit rail lines. Supported

by the banker Charles Tyson Yerkes, the plan proposed by Waddell for the design and construction of the Elevated was published and later realized as the best solution to the problem.

Since 1985 a number of Loop stations have been rebuilt or renovated. The structure at Quincy and Wells has been restored to its 1897 appearance, while those at Washington and Wells, State and Van Buren, and Adams and Wabash have been reassembled, using contemporary materials, and the Clark and Lake station was replaced in 1992. Especially noteworthy at the Adams and Wabash location are the large glassed-in openings that provide a revealing view of the front of the Art Institute a block to the east.

Wieboldt's Annex (1900, 1905)

(Originally Mandel Brothers Annex)

8–14 North Wabash Avenue

ARCHITECTS: Holabird & Roche

Located half a block east of Louis Sullivan's celebrated Carson Pirie Scott Building (22), Wieboldt's Annex bows to it gracefully, forfeiting none of its own intrinsic excellence. While the frame is expressed with a straightforwardness that characterized much of the best turn-of-the-century Chicago commercial architecture, it is instructive to note differing treatments of the frame in this and neighboring buildings. At Carson's, the piers and spandrels are in the same plane, with the windows recessed. In the State Street facade of the Chicago Building (23), the windows together with the spandrels are set behind the piers. In Wieboldt's Annex, a cornice atop each of the spandrels (otherwise on the same plane with the piers) adds a distinctly horizontal emphasis.

The south half of the building was constructed in 1900 to a height of nine stories. The north half went up in 1905, rising eleven stories. At that time, two more floors were added to the south half.

[*16*] **Jewelers' Building** (1882)
15–19 South Wabash Avenue
ARCHITECT: Dankmar Adler

Designed and built while Louis Sullivan was working as a designer-drafts-man in Adler's independent practice, the Jewelers' Building is similar in size and material to commercial buildings constructed in downtown Chicago after the fire of 1871. The Jewelers' Building emphasizes the openness of its facade and demonstrates the character of early Sullivan ornament. These floral forms derive from his study in Paris, his interest in the ideas of conventionalization, and his experience in the office of Philadelphia architect Frank Furness. Despite the unsympathetic ground-floor remodeling, a single original pier can be seen on the north (alley) side of the building. Across the street, Sullivan designed new shop fronts on the first two floors at 18–24. At 10 South Wabash, D. H. Burnham & Company's pressed-brick and green terra-cotta 1897 Silversmith Building was transformed into a boutique hotel in 1998.

Pakula Building (1900)

218 South Wabash Avenue

ARCHITECTS: Holabird & Roche

Built and first named for Boston developer Frederick Ayer, the building quickly became associated with and then named for its major tenant, the bookseller A. C. McClurg & Company. Above the ground-floor shop, the deep, generally open floors served well their open loft functions. As at the Dwight or Carson Pirie Scott Buildings, Holabird & Roche achieved an elegant balance between the horizontality of the Chicago windows and the verticality of its piers. While photographs of the facade tend to suggest a flat and planar facade, in fact the glazed terra-cotta piers are relieved by finely cast flutes, demonstrating that depth in design is more than a matter of measurement.

[*18*] **Page Brothers Building,** also known as the
Loop End Building (1872)
Southeast corner of State and Lake Streets
ARCHITECTS: John Mills van Osdel; State Street facade, Hill &
Woltersdorf (1902)

By contrast with New York City, where cast-iron facades dating mostly
from the late nineteenth century are numerous and highly visible,
Chicago has next to none. They were once plentiful enough here in the
downtown district, thanks largely to the ease with which they could be
prefabricated, cast in the form of details that mimicked a variety of historical styles, and attached to the fronts of buildings with load-bearing
side walls and interior columns. Cast-iron buildings in New York, especially those constructed in lower Manhattan, were mostly left alone, even
often abandoned, after the city's urban action moved uptown. But in
Chicago's smaller central area, there was pressure after the Chicago fire
to put up larger masonry structures and, later still, metal-framed buildings. Thus the chief reason for including the Page Brothers Building in

this text is the rarity of its materials in Chicago, a fact that renders it more important historically than architecturally, but noteworthy nonetheless. When van Osdel designed it, Lake Street was the major downtown commercial street. Since State Street took over the role shortly after the fire, the cast-iron front of the Page Brothers Building facing State was replaced by a new entry and masonry facade by Hill & Woltersdorf in 1902. Thus remodeled, the building has been further rehabilitated, as part the effort to restore the Chicago Theater (19).

[*19*] **Chicago Theater** (1921)
175 North State Street
ARCHITECTS: Rapp & Rapp

The lavish revivalist architecture common to the work of the Chicago-based Rapp brothers and other motion picture theater designers of their time is richly manifest in the adornments of the triumphal arch motif central to the Chicago Theater's State Street facade. Off-white terra-cotta sheathing has been shaped into neo-baroque ornament, while the interior is abundant in French Second Empire decor. The marquee and the six-story vertical sign are later additions.

The movie palace experience that enthralled the nation during the 1920s was neatly rationalized by George Rapp, who wrote: "Watch the eyes of a child as [he] enters the portals of our great theatres and treads the pathway into fairyland. . . . Here is a shrine to democracy where there are no privileged patrons. The wealthy rub elbows with the poor—and are better for this contact." During the last generation, such sentiment has lost much of its idealist gloss, just as the grandiose palaces themselves have been replaced by the shopping mall multiplex. Yet these recent developments, as much as any, have justified preservation of the Chicago Theater, one of the last and best of its breed in the city's downtown area. It is now given over mostly to live performances of popular music.

[**20**] **Marshall Field & Company Store** (1892, 1902, 1906, 1907, 1914)
111 North State Street
ARCHITECTS: On North Wabash Avenue, south section,
D. H. Burnham & Co. (1892); middle section, D. H. Burnham & Co.
(1906); north section, Graham, Burnham & Co. (1914); on North State
Street, north section, D. H. Burnham & Co. (1902); south section,
D. H. Burnham & Co. (1907)

Despite the post–World War II rise of the suburban shopping mall, Marshall Field's downtown store has retained its reputation as one of the world's most famous department store buildings. While it now occupies all of the space of one full block in the Loop, it was erected one section at a time, beginning with the Renaissance palazzo-like portion of 1893 at the northwest corner of Washington Street and Wabash Avenue that served as an annex to an 1879 structure at the northeast corner of State

and Washington Streets. There followed the north half of the State Street front, in 1902; the middle section of the Wabash Avenue front, in 1906; the demolition of the 1879 building and its replacement (by the south half of the State Street front), in 1907; and finally the north section of the Wabash Avenue front, in 1914.

Architect D. H. Burnham and firms bearing his name were responsible for all of this work, with the overall result that the principal portion along State Street closely follows the tendency of turn-of-the-century Chicago commercial builders to express the frame and fill the interstices with horizontal, tripartite Chicago windows. Nonetheless, the architects qualified that usage by referring to classical precedence: three-story base, seven-story shaft topped by an entablature, and a two-story columned attic with a cornice. The State Street entrance is further dramatized by a high portico featuring four Ionic columns on bases, supporting an entablature and a carved balustrade. Two imposing clocks are familiar accoutrements on the State Street corners.

The interior, with its forest of Corinthian columns and polychromed capitals, may come as an impressive surprise. The atrium in the north State Street section rises thirteen stories, while the shorter five-story equivalent in the south section is spanned by a splendidly variegated vault by Louis Comfort Tiffany. The covered delivery driveway that once separated the east and west sections of the building has been filled in, making room for a third atrium, a crossroads of sorts that operates horizontally and vertically, offering the shopper easy access to the rest of the store.

[**21**] **Reliance Building** (1891, 1895)
32 North State Street
ARCHITECTS: Burnham & Root (1891); D. H. Burnham & Co. (1895); restoration, McClier (1999)

Many hands make light work. This monument (basically a speculative office building above street-level shops) of glazed curtain walls rippling over its simple steel frame was constructed in stages. The developer, William Hale, desired a tall building, but only wished four stories at the outset, most of which were to be the upper stories of the existing building, continuously occupied by lease holders. John Wellborn Root designed such a building with spread foundations capable of receiving a tower in the future, but Root died before this work was completed. When the opportunity to continue came, Charles Atwood, then Burnham's chief designer, continued the tower on the existing foundation up to sixteen stories. Demanding clients and ambitious architects and engineers achieved greatness.

Generations of observers learned to see the audacity of this building despite its recent tawdry condition. Finally in 1996 the city of Chicago began the restoration of the Reliance, and it reopened as the Hotel Burnham in 1999. One of the greatest symbols of Chicago as a source of modern architecture is again visible in majestic fact. The cornice has been restored, the terra-cotta cleaned, and lights can now be seen through the clear and clean sheets of glass. The original plate glass has been replaced by insulating double panes of float glass, which are more reflective than transparent, shifting slightly the sense of the glass as a skin that was equally transparent and reflective. As tall buildings are usually seen at an acute angle from below, this distinction is almost without a difference. The pointless interior design of the new hotel suggests figures in thrall to market research rather than the implications of the building's design. Visitors will patiently wait for the next renewal of the interiors for design as strong and good as the exterior.

[*22*] Carson Pirie Scott & Company Building

(1899, 1904, 1906, 1961)
(Originally the Schlesinger and Mayer Store)
1 South State Street, southeast corner of Madison Street
ARCHITECTS: Louis H. Sullivan; addition, D. H. Burnham & Co. (1906); addition, Holabird & Root (1961)

Louis Sullivan's last big building is in four parts. He began with three bays and nine stories on Madison Street. Here the canopy over the sidewalk provides a theatrical entrance to the shopping within. In 1903 and 1904, he extended the building to the corner of State Street and then seven bays down the great street and up to twelve stories with a deeply recessed top floor capped by a thin and strong cornice. In 1948 the cornice was effaced and the recess filled in. In 1906, while Sullivan was still in practice, D. H. Burnham & Company extended the building five more bays along State Street, and in 1960–61 Holabird & Root brought the building to its present form, again extending the facade along State Street three final bays. It is instructive to study the facade at the seam between each section. The lower facade and corner rotunda were restored in 1979 by John Vinci.

The overall composition of the facade draws on Sullivan's idea of the tall building—distinct base, uniform body, strong terminating top. Here

the base offers two levels of large show windows framed by richly ornamented cast-iron plates, which are colored to look like patina bronze. At the corner entrance, the light is richly transmitted by the elaboration of the window surrounds, and the mahogany paneling indicates the quality and dignity of the shopping inside. The white glazed terra-cotta wall planes above the base show the equal importance of pier and spandrel in the structural system and the subsidiary formal place of the windows they frame. The additions have transformed the balance of height and length in Sullivan's sections of the building into a building dominated by its long horizontal dimension. The visual importance of the windows is marked by the subtle elegance of the geometric ornamental patterns in the frames and reveals.

[*23*] **Chicago Building** (1904)

7 West Madison Street

ARCHITECTS: Holabird & Roche

Among the most complete of Holabird & Roche's commercial buildings in the Loop, this building displays its dark red terra-cotta surface above a base recently restored to serve as a dormitory for the School of the Art Institute of Chicago. The facades on State and Madison Streets differ in their composition. On State Street, strong quoined piers at the corners, thin continuous piers in between the three bays, and spandrels recessed behind the piers frame the reflective plane of Chicago windows. Along Madison Street, three bays project ahead of the far simpler ranks of Chicago windows, achieving a prismatic effect for the glass on this facade. Because State Street widens to its north, the Chicago Building's Madison Street facade exploits the offset to present itself to pedestrians walking south along the street.

[*24*] **Second Leiter Building** (1891)

403 South State Street

ARCHITECT: William Le Baron Jenney

Built by Levi Z. Leiter, once a partner of Marshall Field, this is one of the many full-block buildings constructed to mark the dominance of State Street for retail commerce, especially in department stores. (A widely admired First Leiter Building, also by Jenney, was demolished in 1972.) Historians usually praise architect William Le Baron Jenney for the quality and innovation of his engineering, noting his excellent academic training at Harvard's Lawrence Scientific School and in Paris, coupled with his practical experience in support of Grant's western campaign during the Civil War. On the other hand, some of his compositions—such as the Manhattan Building—are enjoyed for their exuberance and variety of detail. Something different occurs at the Second Leiter Building. Although the regular steel frame used here came to imply a unity of facade design, Jenney composed the public facades—Congress Parkway and State and Van Buren Streets—as a unified block of subtly proportioned interrelated elements. A graded sequence of pilasters and spandrels defined and related major and minor elements of the building in connected sequence from the entire composition to the individual window and frame. The powerful stability that this design produces can best be seen today from one of the upper floors of the Harold Washington Library.

[*25*] **Harold Washington Library Center** (1991)
400 South State Street
ARCHITECTS: Hammond, Beeby & Babka

The huge publicity preceding the 1991 opening of the new main Chicago Public Library mostly stemmed from two sources: a long-lasting argument over where the new structure should be erected (indeed, should it be a new building at all or a rehabilitated old one?) and the formal competition for a final design, a contest that unfolded once the South Loop site was selected.

Moreover, the winning entry generated considerable controversy in its own right. Design architect Thomas Beeby conceived a building of the sort one rightly calls an edifice, which mostly looks as if the modernist revolution of the last century had never happened. Clad with granite on the lower levels and brick above, the library is monumental in more than scale, harking back to the Beaux-Arts manner of the late nineteenth cen-

tury not only in its powerful axial symmetry but in the heavy representa-
tional decoration that adorns its exterior. It is clearly indebted to the ancient Western tradition of grandiloquent civic structures.

Yet a closer look confirms that it is a contemporary building after all,
especially in its self-consciously neo-Mannerist mixture of old and new
elements. The whole west wall and the pedimented attic are clad in glass
and aluminum and steel components, whose modernist look is counter-
posed violently but knowingly with the building's overall muscular classicism. The granite base and the attic house the public areas of the library,
the most imposing part of which is the glass-roofed winter garden on the
top story, recently equipped with a restaurant. The undifferentiated stack
spaces of the middle floors are expressed on the facade by tall, deeply
incised arched windows that reinforce the dignity and weight of the
whole. Other latter-day touches are found in the decorative program of
the interior, which features sculptures and paintings by well-known
artists, principally from Chicago.

In his use of ornament, Beeby has expressed his intention to revive
the look of history in a building that, true to the postmodernist aesthetic,
also displays its attachment to contemporaneity. The huge acroteria at
the top edge of the structure feature several representations of the owl,
a bird that stands for wisdom and learning. More specifically, Beeby's

iconography relates to the Midwest and to Chicago. The head of Ceres, Roman goddess of grain, appears in wall medallions together with ears of corn, the pairing symbolic of prairie agriculture. The ninth-floor cornice railing marks the uniform height of buildings proposed in the famous 1909 *Plan of Chicago* of Daniel Burnham and Edward Bennett. And the meaning of "Windy City Man" high on the facade is obvious.

[*26*] **Delaware Building** (1874, 1889)
36 West Randolph Street
ARCHITECTS: Wheelock & Thomas; Julius Huber (1889); restoration, Wilbert Hasbrouck (1982)

This is how the business district of Chicago looked around the time of the 1871 fire. The demand for commercial space just after the fire led architects to reuse existing foundations and forms for building. The facade combines innovation and tradition. It is an early example of the use of precast concrete panels, while the ornamental details of the panels emphasize the heritage of classical architecture—filtered through much space and time. Otis Wheelock studied in the office of New York architect Minard Lafever, whose influential book *The Beauties of Modern Architecture* emphasized mastery of revival forms. The building was constructed in two stages—five stories over a raised basement in 1874, two more stories and the skylighted, steel-frame atrium in 1889. Wilbert Hasbrouck restored the building in 1982, including the soft gray and green color of the facade.

[**27**] **Richard J. Daley Center** (1965)
(Originally the Civic Center)
Block bounded by Randolph, Dearborn, Washington, and Clark Streets
ARCHITECTS: C. F. Murphy Associates; Loebl, Schlossman & Bennett; Skidmore, Owings & Merrill

---

Mies van der Rohe praised this building. Jacques Brownson, chief designer at C. F. Murphy, had studied under Mies at IIT, but Mies admired more than the professional success of a gifted student. Brownson's achievement, first explored in the CNA Building at 55 East Jackson Boulevard, was to combine Mies's two great structural interests in a single building—the long span and the high rise. Mies's Crown Hall (127) is long span, and his 860–880 North Lake Shore Drive (77) is a high-rise. At the Daley Center, Brownson built a tall building that had long spans between the columns—eighty-seven feet from east to west and forty-eight feet from north to south. By comparison, most high-rises then had spans between the columns of about twenty-five to thirty feet.

The practical purpose of the building—to provide large and high courtrooms with no columns interrupting clear sight lines—permitted Brownson to secure a monumental proportional relation between

columns, spandrels, and curtain wall on the exterior. The horizontal emphasis of the long spandrels is offset by the floor-to-floor height, which is about double that of a typical tall office building. (Ordinarily a 650-foot-tall building would be expected to have about sixty stories, not the thirty-one of the Daley Center.) From the interior, these generous proportions provide the spaciousness and grandeur associated with public buildings devoted to justice, though not with modern architecture.

Pablo Picasso's monumental sculpture (fashioned of the same Corten steel as the building) dominates the plaza on the southern half of the building's full block site. Recently redesigned by landscape architect Peter Schaudt, the plaza unites the adjacent city, county, and state buildings.

69 West Washington Street

ARCHITECTS: Skidmore, Owings & Merrill

Several features distinguish the Brunswick Building (now the Cook County Administration Building) from its post–World War II high-rise neighbors. Most notably, it is supported not by the cage of steel columns and beams conventional in tall buildings, but by load-bearing concrete screen

walls and a simple concrete core. Thus the typical office interior has been kept free of columns. Moreover, at the perimeter, loads are passed from the screen walls to only ten perimeter columns via a huge twenty-four-foot-high concrete transfer girder that allows the ground floor to be mostly open to the street at ground level. The mass of the transfer girder is visually reduced by the row of blind openings on its surface. Thus the viewer is led to the single deviation from the dominating rectilinearity of the design, the gentle concave curves at each corner, where the transfer girder and the screen wall meet. This feature was intended to nod to a similar device on the storied Monadnock Building exactly four blocks south on Dearborn Street.

[*29*] **Inland Steel Building** (1958)
30 West Monroe Street
ARCHITECTS: Skidmore, Owings & Merrill

The first tall building to go up in the Loop following the Great Depression, Inland Steel is among the crispest local demonstrations of late modernist style and planning. The office floors in the stainless steel-clad and blue-green glass rectangular tower on the west side of the site are free of columns, since vertical circulation and services are confined within the attached fully metal-clad tower to the east. This interior openness is re-inforced by the placement of the supporting columns outside the exterior wall, which also gives those piers a forceful vertical emphasis. Steel pilings, driven to bedrock eighty-five feet below grade were used here for the first time.

[**30**] **Bank One Building** (1969)
(Originally First National Bank Building)
Madison Street between Dearborn and Clark Streets
ARCHITECTS: Perkins & Will; C. F. Murphy Associates

Tho formal unity perceptible in the buildings of the Loop derives from the steady reliance of the city's designers on the straight line and right angle. In view of that, the sweeping concave curvature of the 850-foot Bank One Building would seem to defy local tradition. Yet it has aged quite well. Most observers have come to judge it among the strongest tall buildings in Chicago, and some have considered the powerful articulation of its walls proof of a bloodline shared with the city's best and boldest commercial structures. Certainly when compared with a pair of similarly composed buildings in Midtown Manhattan, the Bank One Building is a palpably tauter, more muscular work.

Its shape, moreover, is a happy meeting of functional necessity and vigorous, lively form. Since the bank's heaviest public traffic occurs at the lowest levels, these called for the amplest space. Other banking activities require less floor area and are provided for accordingly as the building tapers, while tenants needing still less contiguous space (and demanding premium views) are lodged on upper floors. Meanwhile the interior is freed throughout by the placement of elevators, stairs, and services in cores at each end of the slab. The penthouses that house mechanical and electrical utilities at the crest of the building are divided to repeat the

rhythm of the columns, which in turn extend outward in profile from the exterior walls of granite and bronze-tinted glass.

The plaza at the base of the building is worth comment, since its several levels, dominated by the colorful mosaic *Four Seasons*, by Marc Chagall, have encouraged pedestrian activity and, in the warm months, stimulated a pleasant sociability among the noonday crowd.

[**31**] **Marquette Building** (1895, 1905)

140 South Dearborn Street

ARCHITECTS: Holabird & Roche; westernmost Adams Street bay, Holabird & Roche (1905); McClier Corporation (2002)

Long recognized as a prime example of the celebrated Chicago architectural aesthetic based on the clear expression of the structural frame, the Marquette Building has lately prompted students to study the more traditional aspects of its design. Either approach can be instructive, but the renewed consciousness of the architects' debt to history is worth remarking here. The cornices imposed at various external levels, the rusticated bays at the corners, and the huge cornice atop the attic story— later removed but fortunately restored in 2002, by McClier Corporation— all testify to classical precedent rather than revolutionary modernism. In-

deed, the interior seems almost unqualifiedly devoted to the habits of the past, most evidently in the single Tuscan Doric column in the middle of the foyer, surrounded by a series of colorful mosaics. The latter group together with bronze reliefs above the entrance depict events in the life of Père Marquette, an early French explorer of the Chicago region and the building's namesake. (The artists include Hermon MacNeil, Edward Kemeys, Amy Bradley, and J. A. Holzer.)

All the above notwithstanding, it is the powerful frame, that Chicago specialty, that most commands the eye of the viewer. The asymmetry of the Adams Street facade stems from the 1905 addition of a single bay to the western edge of the original building.

[**32**] **Chicago Federal Center** (1964, 1974, 1991)
Dearborn Street between Jackson Boulevard and Adams Street
ARCHITECTS: Mies van der Rohe; Schmidt, Garden & Erikson; C. F. Murphy Associates; A. Epstein & Sons (1964, 1974); addition, Ralph H. Metcalfe Federal Building (1991), Fujikawa Johnson & Associates

---

The sole work in the Loop by Mies van der Rohe is a complex of three buildings comprising a total large enough to take up much of the space on one full block and a measure of two others. Room is left for a pair of plazas, but the architectural group as a whole is impressively large in any case. The tallest structure is the forty-five-story Kluczynski office building, standing at the south end of the main block and placed there by the architect so that it addresses itself to the main mass of the Loop to the north and more directly to Holabird & Roche's famous Marquette Building (31) across Adams Street. So sited, the Kluczynski also hovers over the main plaza. The low-lying Federal Post Office, a single-story pavilion, occupies the west edge of the block. With S. R. Crown Hall on the campus of Illinois Institute of Technology (127), it is a prime example of the open, universal space that Mies so favored during his American years. To the east, across Dearborn Street, is the thirty-story Dirksen courthouse and office building. The plaza, at grade and mostly unadorned, rewards looking rather than socializing, not only because the buildings relate well

to each other, but because the centerpiece of the ensemble is the scarlet steel *Flamingo* by Alexander Calder, its brilliant color and looping form an effective counterfoil to Mies's sober geometry.

Added in 1991 to a parcel at the southeast corner of Clark and Jackson, across from the smaller plaza (with a sculptural group, *Ruins III*, by Nita Sunderland), is the Ralph H. Metcalfe Federal Building, by Fujikawa Johnson & Associates, its foyer containing a huge metal sculpture, *The Town Ho's Story, with Post Script and the Gam*, by Frank Stella.

[**33**] **William J. Campbell United States Courthouse Annex**
(1975)   (Metropolitan Detention Center)
Van Buren Street between Clark and Federal Streets
ARCHITECTS: Harry Weese Associates

This striking triangular tower, constructed of poured-in-place concrete, serves the Federal Courthouse to the north as a detention and administration center for people being held for trial. Often such detainees have not been convicted of any crime, and so quality of life was an important design consideration. The splayed windows (five inches wide at their narrowest) are the maximum that federal standards will permit without bars.

Ample light and air occurs in the enclosed, landscaped, rooftop exercise yard. Set between every two cell floors are common lounging, dining, and visitors' areas. With its light color (a tawny off-white), distinctive shape, and ground-level landscaped plaza, passersby experience the building as benign rather than forbidding.

[*34*]   **Monadnock Building** (1891, 1893)
53 West Jackson Boulevard
ARCHITECTS: north half, Burnham & Root (1891); south half, Holabird & Roche (1893)

The Monadnock Building, observed nineteenth-century architectural critic Montgomery Schuyler, may be "the thing itself," thus initiating its reputation as a masterpiece of bold simplicity. The slablike form of the

Monadnock, a geological term indicating a freestanding mountain surrounded by a plain, emerges square at grade. The six-foot-thick wall then curves in slightly at the second story and out at its summit, in a subtle echo of the Egyptian pylon. Even more exciting are the rippling bays of the north half of the building, which contrast handsomely with the more prismatic bays of the south half.

Using four sections to better serve the interests of the developers, Burnham & Root established the overall plan and built the northern two sections using bearing-wall construction, which accounts in part for its

distinctive expression. Holabird & Roche designed the southern two sections, expressing them as a metal frame, although the recent restoration of the building has shown that even the northern half of this work uses outer bearing walls. Originally each section had its own name, taken from a New England mountain. From north to south it was Monadnock, Kearsarge (both in New Hampshire), Wachusetts (in Massachusetts), and Katahdin (in Maine).

[**35**] **Fisher Building** (1896, 1907)
343 South Dearborn Street
ARCHITECTS: D. H. Burnham & Co.; northern addition,
Peter J. Weber (1907)

Although the Gothic appears both early and late in the history of Chicago commercial building, it is important to note a major difference in overall shape of the Fisher Building and Howells & Hood's Tribune Tower of 1925 (67). The latter is accurately named, a tower clearly tall and aspiring. The former, however much it shares with the Tribune Tower both vertical thrust and Gothicized ornamentation, is a rectangular prism, less searchingly tall, and, as such, anatomically close to the Chicago office buildings of the 1890s.

That said, the Fisher is worth close scrutiny for its elegant use of oriel windows, engaged colonnettes at its corner piers, and the visual puns on its name that appear on the outer walls.

[**36**] **Old Colony Building** (1894)
407 South Dearborn Street
ARCHITECTS: Holabird & Roche

The most fetching features of the Old Colony Building are its round projecting corners, popular among architects of the time for several advantages: internally, they are meant to create desirable office spaces, well illuminated and with cross-ventilation. Moreover, they add interest to the profile of the building, which further warrants inclusion here as the last remaining downtown structure so designed.

The Old Colony has other merits as well, less obvious but no less effective. The row of vertical piers on the Dearborn Street side effectively balances the width of that facade, while in contrast, the narrow Van Buren Street elevation gains an illusion of breadth by virtue of the continuous horizontality of its spandrels.

The Old Colony is also noteworthy as engineering. It was the first tall building in which a problem common to all skeletally framed high-rises, stiffening against the wind, was addressed by a system of internal portal arches. Portal bracing, derived from bridge construction, appeared in the construction of tall structures during the early 1880s, but the arched form at Old Colony was an innovation.

[*37*] **Manhattan Building** (1891)

431 South Dearborn Street

ARCHITECTS: William Le Baron Jenney; renovation, Hasbrouck/Hunderman (1982)

The distinguished early history of building in Chicago cannot be fairly written if confined to the accomplishments of people known chiefly as architects. Engineers were no less vital to the construction of the city, and among them no one stands higher than William Le Baron Jenney. Proof enough of his inventiveness is apparent in his Manhattan Building, which was one of the earliest high-rise office buildings to employ the skeletal frame throughout. The complicated facade is less universally admired, but it has its champions, who enjoy its amiable assortment of forms and often cite the charm of the grotesque faces carved in the trumps of the bays. The Manhattan was renovated by Hasbrouck/Hunderman in 1982, at which time it was converted to residential use.

Printers Row   *(entries 38–40)*

Three blocks of Dearborn Street south from Congress Parkway to the tower of the Dearborn Street Station give the district its focus. They were developed over three decades from the 1880s to the 1910s. High-speed presses and efficient rail distribution of their products led many printing and publishing businesses to locate in this area. The powerful frames and freight elevators of the buildings, along with efficient use of natural and artificial lighting, permitted the vertical integration of all printing tasks within the same structure. Typically, the presses were placed in the basement, independent commercial shops faced the street on the first floor, and other tasks—binding, shipping, administration—occupied the upper stories. Often space on the upper floors was rented to others in the trade.

   Chicago, with its highly competitive printing industry, was also a national center for the graphics trade. As a result of this and because these buildings flank a street that runs between an important rail passenger station and the commercial center in the Loop, many of the facades received more attention and finer materials than structures for similar purposes on less prominent sites. These facades tended to reflect contemporaneous architectural tastes—whether the H. H. Richardson–influenced Donohue & Henneberry Building, the Chicago school exemplar Pontiac Building, or the richly and persuasively eclectic Lakeside Press Building (now the Columbia College Residence Center). In this last building, as in Nimmons's New Franklin Building, Howard Van Doren Shaw developed images and motifs illustrating the history and character of printing. Chicago artist Oskar Gross designed the tile mosaics on the New Franklin Building. Regardless of the materials used or the architectural tradition being recalled or developed, the facades are clearly and powerfully articulated, and in studying the proportions of window and wall, the architects most often gave preference to the open spaces of the windows.

Printers Row lost much of its functional identity in the years following World War II. Improvements in technology favored the major printing companies that could afford newer, more sophisticated equipment and larger plants. Smaller companies were taken over in the process or forced out of business, and the local printing industry became less centralized. Moreover, the railroads ceased to be the best means of transporting printed goods. By the 1970s many of the old spaces along South Dearborn Street were empty. Later they were gradually turned into loft apartments, some of them among the earliest examples in Chicago of a genre that has become an increasingly popular residential form in the late twentieth and early twenty-first century townscape.

47 West Polk Street

ARCHITECTS: Cyrus L. W. Eidlitz; conversion, Kaplan McLaughlin Diaz and Hasbrouck/Hunderman (1986); Vinci-Hamp (1995)

In its present state, Dearborn Street Station is fully recognizable as the building designed by architect Eidlitz (whose offices were in New York), but two major changes have significantly altered both the exterior and interior. A fire in 1922 robbed the head house of the original steeply pitched, ornately tiled roofs, replete with dormers, that added both richness and charm to its profile. The building is now perceptibly more earthbound. Moreover, in 1986, long after it had ceased to function as a railroad terminal, the station was turned into a combination shopping mall and commercial offices. Kaplan McLaughlin Diaz of San Francisco, with Hasbrouck/Hunderman, supervised that second renovation. In 1995 the shop fronts and canopies on the Polk Street facade were added by Vinci-Hamp.

These considerable alterations notwithstanding, Dearborn Street Station remains a substantial piece of work, partly because the excellent ornamental detailing of the redbrick walls and granite base does justice to Eidlitz's overall reference to the Romanesque, and hardly less because of the building's fortunate site. Visible at the south end of Dearborn Street,

it is a fitting conclusion to a thoroughfare lined with more important commercial structures than any other in Chicago.

[**39**] **Columbia College Residence Center** (1897, 1902)
(Originally the Lakeside Press Building)
731 South Plymouth Court
ARCHITECTS: Howard Van Doren Shaw; conversion, Shayman, Salk, Arenson, Sussholz & Co. (1993)

The special gifts of architect Howard Van Doren Shaw are amply manifest in a building that was originally the home of the Lakeside Press, R. R. Donnelley & Co. That Shaw was fundamentally a traditionalist, with special sympathies for the Arts and Crafts movement, is evident enough here in his use of the round arch and the classical detailing he added to the corners, and surely in the pleasure he took in adding such surface ornamentation as the medallions at the top of the piers and the reliefs at the entrance. The latter include a coat-of-arms, with an Indian head, a depiction of Fort Dearborn, and assorted references to books published by the Lakeside Press.

Nonetheless, Shaw managed to incorporate these devices convincingly into the package of an urban commercial building. Especially noteworthy in this respect is the industrialized look of the undecorated windows and the recessed metallic spandrels of the main shaft of the facade. In 1902 Shaw added four bays to the north.

After the Lakeside Press gave up the building, the interior was converted into apartments. In 1993 Columbia College took over ownership, whereupon the firm of Shayman, Salk, Arenson, Sussholz & Company converted the entire structure into a residential hall for the college's students.

[**40**] **Pontiac Building** (1891)
542 South Dearborn Street
ARCHITECTS: Holabird & Roche; renovation, Booth Hansen Associates (1985)

The oldest surviving downtown building by Holabird & Roche, the Pontiac was erected in the same year as the celebrated Monadnock Building (34) a few blocks to the north, also on Dearborn Street. The similarity in the two works suggested by their common use of oriel windows is not borne out structurally. The Monadnock is a bearing-wall building, while the Pontiac has a skeletal frame. Yet at the same time, since the oriels of the east and west facades of the Pontiac span two structural bays, the presence of the vertical member behind each is concealed on the exterior. While the unqualified expression of the frame is one of the features most asso-

ciated with the Chicago school of the 1890s, Holabird & Roche, in this case unburdened by such foreknowledge, seem to have been exploring the expression of the wall as a thin and flexible membrane.

The original ground-floor facade was replicated in the 1985 renovation by Booth Hansen Associates.

~~~~~~~~~~~~

[*41*] **Dwight Building** (1911)
626 South Clark Street
ARCHITECTS: Schmidt, Garden & Martin

This simple concrete-framed commercial loft building shows why Hugh Garden, principal designer of his firm, is so admired. The enclosing brick

of the facade is presented as a uniformly flat plane. Modest horizontal ornamental strips, with vaselike ornaments over the piers, projected slightly at the top and bottom of the loft floors. While the upper-level ornament has been masked, the minimal, lion-faced capitals of the ground-level piers carry a thin, tautly interlaced course of ornament. Window units are set within this carefully proportioned frame. They exploit the Chicago window type by framing the mullions in an echo of the overall composition of the facade.

LaSalle Street Canyon *(entries 42–48)*

At the core of the Loop is the LaSalle Street canyon, focusing with great intensity on the base and tower of Holabird & Root's Chicago Board of Trade Building. Unlike the other ensembles in the city's central area, which derive their effect from either natural elements (the lakefront for the Michigan Avenue cliff and the river for the Michigan Avenue Bridge group and the riverfront overall) or zones of interchange (the rail terminal on Printers Row), the LaSalle Street canyon derives its power from the exploitation of a rare event in the city's gridded plan. The city's grid, particularly in the Loop, is based on the square block. This means that, on its flat site, one can regularly look along a street, flanked by very tall buildings, and still see, whether over the lake or the prairie, a great pool of light that exists at the end of the compressed vista.

Since the nineteenth century, the Chicago Board of Trade Building has closed such a vista at the foot of LaSalle Street. Here is the commercial and speculative heart of the city. The Chicago Board of Trade tower faces north and is thus almost always seen in shadow or artificially illuminated, intensifying the character of the street. In addition, LaSalle Street narrows in several steps as it approaches the Chicago Board of Trade, and this forces the perspective that enhances the power of the canyon. The narrow Savings of America Tower at 120 North LaSalle, by Helmut Jahn, is only the most recent building to use this condition to powerful effect.

The quality and variety of shadow along LaSalle Street, where the probity of large conservative law firms blends with the raw speculation of traders in the exchanges, have most recently been represented in the only Chicago building to bear the hand of Philip Johnson, who collaborated with Chicago native John Burgee on its design. Their 190 South LaSalle Building is a shade of another sort, wherein the building's form recalls the long-demolished Masonic Temple of 1892 by Burnham &

Root, while its elevations recall the punched-opening masonry walls of modernist buildings of the 1950s.

Just north of the Board of Trade are the facing pediments of the Federal Reserve and Bank of America Center. Reflecting an ancient hierarchy, the Federal Reserve uses the Corinthian order for its columns, while the Bank of America acknowledges its slightly lower status by using the Ionic order. Both, however, defer to the Art Deco form of the Board of Trade, defining as it does the central private economic power of the city. They also complete the compression and narrowing of the street by having the only porticoes that project from the building mass. Just as the vertical edges of the street's buildings appear to step down as they approach the tower of the Chicago Board of Trade, so do the porticoes of the banks participate in a series of horizontal steps rising from the street to the porticoes to the refined and abstracted planar pediment of the Chicago Board of Trade entrance block. This is capped by two carved figures of Trade (who create a split acroteria) and terminates, finally, against the sky in the pyramidal cap of the great center tower.

Chicago Board of Trade Building (1930, 1982, 1997)

141 West Jackson Boulevard

ARCHITECTS: Holabird & Root (1930); additions, Murphy/Jahn, Shaw & Associates, and Swanke Hayden Connell (1982); Fujikawa Johnson & Associates (1997)

The Chicago Board of Trade Building is a powerful termination to the LaSalle Street canyon, achieving its force through a low entry pavilion containing trading pits over the entrance. Setbacks rise above this, and behind is the forty-five-story tower, whose pyramidal top is capped by John Storrs's statue of Ceres, all thirty-one aluminum feet of the goddess of grain. Alvin Meyer's low-relief carvings of an Indian holding corn and a Mesopotamian holding wheat flank the clock over the entrance and indicate that two of the staffs of life form the basis of the frenzied activities within. Throughout Holabird & Root exploited the fluidity of Art Deco in the composition and ornament of the building.

W. W. Boyington's earlier Board of Trade building occupied the site from 1885 to 1929. The title action of Frank Norris's 1903 novel *The Pit* took place in that sphinx of a building. The trading pits within the 1930 building and its additions testify to the adaptability of the traders to new forms of commodities and other instruments of trade. Electronic trading now challenges the future role of the open outcry system of setting prices, which the pits embody.

Helmut Jahn's 1983 addition is his first building to explore the tensions of mimicking masonry forms with thin curtain walls. Here he has taken the tower of the original Board of Trade, made it shorter and fatter for programmatic purposes, added it to the back of the original building like a bustle, and then capped his new pyramid with an octagonal element that symbolizes the trading pits of the exchanges. A more ordinary reading of the form suggests the hoods and radiator ornaments of the luxury cars driven by exchange traders in earlier years.

[*43*] **Bank of America Center** (1924)
231 South LaSalle Street
ARCHITECTS: Graham, Anderson, Probst & White

The Bank of America Center—first constructed for the Illinois Merchants Bank, later housing the Continental Illinois National Bank—presents a powerful pedimented Ionic portico to LaSalle Street and a reserved, discretely detailed limestone mass as it fills out its block in the center of the city's financial district. The Bank of America Center and the higher-status (expressed through the use of the Corinthian order at the entrance) Federal Reserve Bank across LaSalle Street, also by Graham, Anderson, Probst & White, framed the vista to the 1885 Chicago Board of Trade by W. W. Boyington, a building that came to be dwarfed by the younger giants around it. Graham, Anderson, Probst & White's buildings demonstrated their anticipation of the redevelopment of the Board of Trade with a larger building whose scale would be influenced by the context they

provided. Above the ground-level shops of the interior arcade, the great banking floor, flanked with grand Ionic colonnades, provides a space of imperial splendor. Above the colonnades and below the deeply coffered ceiling is a cycle of murals by Jules Guerin. His theme is the peoples of the world, and he sets them in an environment of buildings and spaces derived from the World's Columbian Exposition, Chicago's 1893 World's Fair.

[*44*] **Rookery Building** (1888)

209 South LaSalle Street

ARCHITECTS: Burnham & Root; renovations, Frank Lloyd Wright (1907); William B. Drummond (ca. 1930); restoration, McClier (1992)

With the Monadnock, the Rookery epitomizes the qualities of the Burnham & Root partnership. Rich and flexible in design, sophisticated and responsive in planning, intelligent and innovative in structure and use of

materials, the whole displays an enormous self-confidence. Not only does the building present a compelling solution to the problem of the large office building; it also suggests alternative possibilities. This is most richly expressed on the ground floor, where the power of rusticated red-granite walls, the elegance of polished red-granite columns, and the taut fragility of the windows combine for a seemingly effortless grand effect. Further enhanced by Frank Lloyd Wright's reworking of the atrium in white marble and William Drummond's elevator lobbies, a decade-long cleaning and restoration of the building was magnificently completed by McClier in 1992, following prior work by Hasbrouck/Hunderman, Hasbrouck Peterson Associates, and Booth Hansen Associates. A small patch of original floor mosaic may be seen adjacent to an original Burnham & Root column in the lobby.

[**45**] **135 South LaSalle Street** (1934)
(Formerly LaSalle National Bank Building; originally the Field Building)
ARCHITECTS: Graham, Anderson, Probst & White

The edifice at 135 South LaSalle is that Chicago rarity: a building excellent enough to justify the demolition of a comparably important structure to make room for it: William Le Baron Jenney's Home Insurance Building of 1885, a work notable as the world's first tall building to employ an all-metal structural frame. The LaSalle, if less technically innovative than Jenney's effort, is aesthetically superior. While conceived and executed in the Art Deco manner, it is an exceptionally svelte, purified example of the style. The reticent classicism of the LaSalle Street frontispiece is expressed in elegant materials securely proportioned. Much the same can be said of the ground-floor foyer, whose dry palette of white, beige, and green marble, reinforced by sleek metal fixtures and mirrored surfaces, makes the very act of walking through the main corridor a refreshing experience.

The exterior consists of a slender forty-three-story slab flanked by a quartet of twenty-two-story towers at its corners, "five towering edifices in one," as it has been called. The suppressed spandrels reinforce the verticality of the building as it rises relatively ornament-free from the pavement.

The LaSalle was the last major building to be completed in the Loop until the Inland Steel Building went up in 1958. The Great Depression and World War II had intervened, and a visit to the building still summons the bittersweet memory that it was designed in the late 1920s, when American economic optimism was at its crest, but completed at a time when the national mood was all too grievously reversed.

[*46*] **Savings of America Tower** (1992)
120 North LaSalle Street
ARCHITECTS: Murphy/Jahn

For some time Helmut Jahn has been exploring the relationship between the massiveness of stone-clad office buildings and the lightness of the structural frame enclosed with a curtain wall. Here, on a tight, relatively

narrow midblock site, he has used stone to convey weight and curtain wall to convey lightness to stunning effect. The building is most notable from the street for its large mosaic by Roger Brown, *The Flight of Daedalus and Icarus*. For such a slim rectangular site, Jahn has introduced substantial curves on every axis—at the top, in the mosaic, and, most effectively, as the device to exploit the progressive narrowing of LaSalle Street toward the Chicago Board of Trade.

[*47*] **City Hall–County Building** (1911)
Block bounded by LaSalle, Randolph, Clark, and Washington Streets
ARCHITECTS: Holabird & Roche

Chicago's Loop gained in two pronounced ways after the creation of the Civic Center (now Daley Center) Plaza in the 1960s. The first was the construction, completed in 1965, of the celebrated Richard J. Daley Center itself (27), designed by C. F. Murphy Associates. But there was a bonus: the very opening of the plaza, which provided an unprecedentedly generous view of City Hall, a building impressive not only by itself, but as a splendid spatial backdrop. City Hall displays a power akin to that of the Daley Center, but more because its neoclassicism marks it as stylistically different from rather than similar to the Daley Center's Mies-influenced modernism.

City Hall's date of 1911 is a reminder that shortly before World War I Chicago architecture turned from the declarative manner practiced in the 1890s, especially by Holabird & Roche, to more pointedly historical styles. The twelve-story mass is relieved by rows of giant Corinthian columns that divide a three-story base from a bold attic level. The exterior is clad mostly in granite, with green terra-cotta (posing as bronze) in some of the window bays.

The lobby of the building, with its vaulted ceilings covered in mosaic, is one of the handsomest interior spaces in Chicago. A near-regal extravagance reminds the viewer that politics is the lifeblood of the city and Cook County, and this building is clearly the heart that pumps it.

James R. Thompson Center (1985)

(Originally the State of Illinois Center)

Block bounded by Randolph, LaSalle, Lake, and Clark Streets

ARCHITECTS: Murphy/Jahn

The Thompson Center has been by far the most controversial yet engrossing building erected in the Loop during the past several decades. The issues of the debate surrounding it are not only aesthetic and practical but political as well. Formally, the building's huge, sloping, aggressively curvilinear mass, mounted by a diagonally truncated glass cylinder, deviates strikingly from the prevailing rectilinearity of Chicago's downtown architecture. To some observers, Helmut Jahn's design is a powerfully original invention, to others, a contextual blasphemy. Functionally, because the exterior is predominantly glass, the heating and ventilation system has never fully protected the seventeen-story atrium space against interior temperature fluctuations. Complaints about noise persist from employees who work in the partition-free offices bordering the atrium.

Whether the Thompson Center is a spectacular extravagance reflective of the clamorous ambitions of the Illinois governor who promoted it and for whom it was renamed (it was originally the State of Illinois Center), or a brilliantly original work made possible by the same man's courageous patronage, the building has always had a riveting public presence. It attracts attention by its very siting across from the Chicago City Hall and the Daley Center, two other buildings of architectural note and governmental import. Sight lines from the plaza of the Daley Center make it especially visible. Its massive southwest-to-northeast curve is fronted by a row of large freestanding granite posts that converge on an abstract sculpture by Jean Dubuffet (cheerfully dubbed by the public "Snoopy in a Blender") at the northwest corner of Randolph and Clark Streets. The north and west facades are flat and less interesting, although references to classical devices point to a connection with the postmodernist aesthetic.

In the interior all but the lower stories are open to the atrium. Elevators and stairs also cantilever into that space, producing the vision of a concave surface seen by some as dazzling, by others as cacophonous. A

large circular opening in the street-level floor leads downward one story to refectory services. Color abounds throughout, adding further to one of the most visually arresting architectural phenomena in the city.

~~~~~~~~~~~~

[*49*] Brooks Building (1910)
223 West Jackson Boulevard
ARCHITECTS: Holabird & Roche

The Brooks Building is seldom singled out as one of the city's masterpieces, but its special value rests in the very fact that it is a typical Chicago work of high quality and almost flawless composition. The skeletal frame has rarely been expressed more directly, more in keeping with Chicago tradition. Much the same can be said of the horizontal window, although here it consists of three sashes rather than the more frequent two flanking a large single fixed light. The building is also notable for the flourishes of ornament at attic level, which confirm the domination of the verticality of the clustered piers over the recessed spandrels.

[**50**] **AT&T Corporate Center and USG Building** (1988, 1992)
227 West Monroe Street and 125 South Franklin Street
ARCHITECTS: Skidmore, Owings & Merrill

Metaphorically, postmodernist architecture wants to have its cake and eat it too. For inspiration it glances to history, especially historical decorative schemes, yet it continues to embrace the abstraction-derived simplicity associated with classic modernism. The AT&T Center and the USG Building, two high-rises connected at the base, were creations of the 1980s, the decade when postmodernism guided the thinking of many architects, and it looks the part. The taller of the two towers rises in several setbacks, bringing to mind similar usages in the high-rises of the late 1920s, and its immense multipart balconied foyer is alive with ornament. The floors are elaborate with patterns in granite and marble, the walls with richly crafted wood; and the entire interior is lit by sumptuous chandeliers. Nonetheless, the generally crisp decor steers clear of fussiness, and the past is remembered without being imitated. This is one of the best efforts by the Chicago Skidmore office that postdates the generation of architects identified with the Hancock Center and the Sears Tower.

[*51*] **Union Station** (1925)

Canal Street between Adams Street and Jackson Boulevard

ARCHITECTS: Graham, Burnham & Co. (1913–17); Graham, Anderson, Probst & White (after 1917)

Union Station, designed and completed by his successors, was Daniel Burnham's dream of helping resolve the chaos of rail passenger traffic in Chicago. He devoted an entire chapter of his 1909 *Plan of Chicago* to the

problems of railroads in the city. The facility is both a station (some tracks go through) and a terminal (some tracks end here). Only two-thirds of the original complex survives—the track structures and passenger circulation and baggage handling functions underground, and to the west the head house, with a great waiting room at its heart, surrounded by services and offices. The head house foundations were designed to carry a taller office building, and plans for such are advanced now and then. A great Doric colonnade of Bedford limestone marks the entrance to the building along Canal Street, while the waiting room has a grand scale, with niches, great columns, vaulted ceiling, and classical detail, derived from the example of ancient Roman baths.

Missing since 1969 is the dramatic arrival hall or concourse, replaced by nondescript buildings. The arrival hall was a great vessel of light—not surprisingly as it was patterned after the similar space (also destroyed) at New York's Pennsylvania Station—centered transversely above the tracks, where arriving passengers were directed by the axis of the concourse and its great windows west to the Union Station head house and east, along narrow Quincy Street, to the dome of Henry Ives Cobb's 1905 Federal Building.

In his film *The Untouchables*, Brian De Palma pays homage to the scene on the Odessa steps in Sergei Eisenstein's *Potemkin*, filming on the northern flight of stairs from the waiting room to Canal Street.

[*52*] **St. Patrick's Church** (1856, 1885)
718 West Adams Street
ARCHITECTS: Carter & Bauer; restoration, Booth Hansen Associates (1992–)

Begun in 1853, dedicated in 1856, west of the path of, and thus not damaged by, the great fire of 1871, this church has been richly embellished, nearly abandoned, and currently survives as the city's oldest church structure. Its towers were added in 1885. Thomas O'Shaughnessy designed its art glass after studying the Book of Kells, the justly celebrated eighth-century Irish illuminated manuscript of the four New Testament Gospels in the library of Trinity College, Dublin. O'Shaughnessy worked at

St. Patrick's between 1912 and 1922, and his windows were restored from 1992 to 1995. In addition to the windows, Booth Hansen Associates also restored interior colors and stencils, as well as the central gable of the facade. At one recent point having a congregation of only four, it has grown again as the neighborhood parish of new middle-class residents of the west Loop. Its exterior form is simple to the point of austerity. The evidence of the respect and care of generations of congregants testifies to its importance to this part of the city as a starting point for immigrants. St. Patrick's also retains significant archives and artifacts of the building's prior decorative schemes, paralleling the city's history.

The Chicago Riverfront and
Wacker Drive *(entries 53–65)*

The visual axis of the main branch of the Chicago River when approached from Lake Michigan is starkly terminated by the black east elevation of Mies van der Rohe's IBM Building with a force like that of the slab that keeps popping up in Stanley Kubrick's *2001: A Space Odyssey*. The main and south branches of the river in the Loop are the city's psychic main street, where the dreams of Chicagoans flow from deep within the city to join the ambition, desire, and fantasy of the center. Today the river corridor approaches the completion of a vision begun with plans for the riverfront in Burnham's 1909 *Plan of Chicago*. The city's numerous bridges and strip parks along the river edge provide a public context for a sequence of buildings of unfolding power and drama, which address both the river and the skyline. Just as Mies's IBM marks the gateway to the river and the city, Kohn Pedersen Fox's 333 West Wacker Drive marks the turn from the main to the south branch of the river. Two elements often claimed to be destructive of urban qualities and values—modern architecture and the American urban grid—have here provided urbane gestures that benefit the city's form enormously. In some cases, architects have designed background buildings for the foreground sites of the riverfront, as in the efforts of Ricardo Bofill and Kevin Roche at 77 and 35 West Wacker, respectively. On the other hand, the slightly jumpy assertiveness of the Morton International Building provides as rewarding a solution to a difficult site as the more relaxed Daily News Building to its south.

East and West Wacker Drive border the south side of the main branch of the river before turning south, where North and South Wacker Drive have been developed as a wide boulevard of towers one block east of the south branch of the river. The emergence of cars from and their disappearance into Lower Wacker Drive is exciting for its unexpect-

edness. The buildings on the west side of Wacker Drive enjoy frontage on the river. Many of them exploit this dual quality, often by inserting pedestrian passages along the river's edge. Wacker Drive was completed in 1926, and the city began a reconstruction of the two-level thoroughfare in early 2001. Wacker Drive has demonstrated its efficiency in distributing traffic throughout its life, and the enhancement of its river edge as a series of broad pedestrian walkways giving access to the river has won the acclaim of visitors and residents alike.

Block bounded by Franklin Street, Wacker Drive, Adams Street, and Jackson Boulevard

ARCHITECTS: Skidmore, Owings & Merrill; Wacker Drive atrium addition, Skidmore, Owings & Merrill (1985); Wacker Drive canopy, Franklin Street canopy, and skydeck lobby, DeStefano & Partners (1992)

When the Sears Tower was completed, it received considerable attention, since at 1,454 feet and 110 stories, it was recognized as the tallest building in the world. The architectural critics, however, delivered mixed reviews, a fact worth citing, since by virtual consensus the building has meanwhile grown mightily in the estimation of the professionals, so that now it is customarily regarded as one of the city's finest buildings.

The compliments have persisted even as the building was surpassed in height by the Petronas Towers in Kuala Lumpur. Height nonetheless is altogether relevant to the Sears design, since the setbacks that define its profile give life to a mass that without them might easily amount to a pillar of boredom. Moreover, the great shaft, sheathed in black anodized aluminum and bronze-tinted glass, depends upon the use of the tubular frame, a construction system in which the vertical supports are kept close enough to each other that the wall of the tube, rather than the more conventional and more expensive interior cage, bears the load. The Sears Tower is so tall that its resistance to wind requires nine such tubes, each seventy-five feet square and all of them bundled together as they grow to their individual heights. Obviously there are more at the bottom than at the top, since the business activities of the Sears owners required more space than those of the tenant occupants of the higher floors. (This functional necessity accounts for a similar "tapering" design in the Bank One Building [30] and the John Hancock Center [74]).

The nine tubes of the Sears Tower rise to a common height of forty-nine stories, whereupon the plan settles into a Z shape for the next sixteen stories. At the sixty-fifth floor, the southwest and northeast tubes terminate and the shaft continues as a cruciform to the base of the ninetieth floor. At that point the north, east, and south tubes stop, leaving a rectangular tower to continue twenty stories to the full height. Central

to the design of the building was the collaboration between the lead architect, Bruce Graham, and the chief engineer, Fazlur Khan.

As at the Federal Center (32), the American sculptor Alexander Calder was commissioned to create a monumental artwork for the Sears Tower, in this case the whimsical *Universe*, a moving wall piece that adorns the foyer. The building deserves a better setting than the uninspired granite plaza it occupies. The entrance has been redone several times. The current canopies were designed by the Chicago firm of DeStefano & Partners.

[*54*] **Hartford Plaza North and South** (1961, 1971)
100 & 150 South Wacker Drive
ARCHITECTS: Skidmore, Owings & Merrill

This pair of well-designed buildings, erected a decade apart at the river's edge, illustrates the modernist challenge of the foreground building. The midcentury desire of Skidmore, Owings & Merrill to express in the façade

the character (in this case uniformity) of the office building collides with the possibilities of the riverside site, which is enriched by such older edifices as Riverside Plaza (originally the Chicago Daily News Building). Although there is a pedestrian passage at the water's edge, the facades are as reticent as the office floors they frame. The single grace note is in the earlier northern building, where a finely detailed concrete frame (note the slight haunchlike swelling where beams meet columns) projects ahead of the office-enclosing glass, providing visual relief and interest to the street and shade to the office occupants.

[**55**] **Civic Opera Building** (1929)
20 North Wacker Drive
ARCHITECTS: Graham, Anderson, Probst & White

Virtually everything visible and invisible about the Civic Opera Building is impressive: the complexity of its structure and functional parts, the opulence of its decor, and, not least, its history. It was put up at the behest

mostly of Chicago financier Samuel Insull, who, following the multiuse precedent of the Auditorium Building (2), meant it to include an opera house and a smaller theater as well as enough office space to fill a sky-scraper-sized building. The very act of incorporating a pair of theaters of differing sizes within so great a volume required a truss system suffi-ciently sophisticated to ensure the transfer of loads at a variety of levels. The subsequent assignment of ornamenting the theaters as well as the surfaces of the building's exterior was also carried out in masterly fash-ion. The color throughout the interior is brilliant, and the decorative form unique in its negotiation of a style recognizably Art Deco but distinctly more dependent on the classical vocabulary than most work in that manner.

The theaters are surmounted by a lofty forty-five-story-high central tower that overlooks two flanking wings. The west elevation resembles an enormous throne, while the east elevation is notable for the covered monumental colonnade that runs along North Wacker Drive.

[**56**] **Riverside Plaza** (1929)
(Originally the Chicago Daily News Building)
400 West Madison Street
ARCHITECTS: Holabird & Root

Originally the home of the *Chicago Daily News* and now given over exclusively to private offices and businesses, Riverside Plaza was the first major building in Chicago to be erected on air rights over railroad tracks, and the first in which a public plaza was considered part of the whole package. The plaza, which fronts the Chicago River looking across to the Civic Opera Building, is spacious and rather grand, a point worth making, or rather lamenting, since it has never been the potentially sociable space it deserves to be.

The building is a prime example of the so-called setback style, in which the building mass is recessed at certain points as it rises from the ground. Begun in New York as a means of narrowing the mass of tall buildings, thus keeping them from blocking light to the streets below, it took on the character of a formal style in the 1920s. Riverside Plaza follows the formula in a memorably creative way, as is evident from vertical as well as horizontal notches that invigorate the main slab and the organization of the two wings.

A corridor in the southern wing connecting the plaza to the Metra station in Citicorp Center was long notable for the ceiling mural by John Norton that illustrated the activities of a great daily newspaper. Almost a decade has passed since the mural was removed by the owners of the building, who presumably intended to have it restored. Since the owners have answered all queries about the fate of the mural by the observation that its restoration would be "very costly," the art and architectural community of Chicago now despairs of its eventual return.

[**57**] **Citicorp Center** (1987)
500 West Madison Street
ARCHITECTS: Murphy/Jahn

Sited among the cluster of high-rise structures that have quickened growth along the west edge of the downtown business district, this building was achieved only at the price of losing one of the great Guastavino-vaulted buildings of the early twentieth century, the old Chicago and North Western Station. Most of the 1.6 million square feet of the new building are allocated to office floors, while the lower reaches contain

the new terminal facilities. To reawaken the sense of the vast interior that so distinguished the former building, Murphy/Jahn have here created a lobby eighty feet high, with eighty thousand square feet of floor area bordered by shops and standard terminal accoutrements. The space is mammoth, made palpably more so by the powerful play of structural beams and columns that make a strong first—or last—impression of architectural Chicago on anyone arriving in or departing from the city.

100 North Riverside Plaza
ARCHITECTS: Perkins & Will

The conscious bow to the riverfront made on the colonnaded and land-scaped east side of this building is the most obvious evidence of an awareness of physical context, while such lesser but noteworthy ancient devices as a clock tower and a marble-clad lobby recall skyscrapers of 1910–20. Nonetheless, all of these elements are carried out in strongly structural rectilinearity reminiscent of Chicago's traditional commercial architecture. The frame remains vigorously expressed, although it appears in a variety of forms. Even a roof truss from which the southern extension is suspended brings to mind comparable devices used by Mies van der Rohe.

333 West Wacker Drive (1983)

ARCHITECTS: Kohn Pedersen Fox

The union of this building's site and form creates a rare architectural drama. Thrusting up from the sharp turn of the Chicago River at the northwest corner of the central business district, its 365-foot-wide curving, green-tinted reflective glass facade is strikingly visible from the rail and auto lines that lead from the North Side into the downtown area. In that sense, it is an arresting monolithic gatepost signaling the center of the city, while the serrated angles of its street side, or southeast, elevation are in comparable accord with the denser environment of the Loop.

This is the first Chicago building by Kohn Pedersen Fox and the only one by that New York firm realized mostly in the modernist mode. The

firm adopted a postmodernist idiom for its several later commissions downtown. Even so, a hint of postmodern historicism and an intentional ambiguity currently labeled double coding is evident here in the neo–Art Deco striped marble that distinguishes the lowest of the thirty-six stories from the minimalist surfaces of its upper ranges. The differentiation of the base from the office floors above it has a functional rationale as well: it houses the building's mechanical facilities.

[**60**] **Merchandise Mart** (1931)
Chicago River (north bank) between Wells and Orleans Streets
ARCHITECTS: Graham, Anderson, Probst & White

Built by Marshall Field & Company to replace and expand in function H. H. Richardson's Marshall Field Wholesale Store, this very large build-ing—only the Pentagon is supposed to be larger in floor area—continues to serve as the great central market for contract furnishings. Jules Guerin's cycle of murals in the main lobby highlights the relation of Chicago to other commercial entrepôts throughout the world. Graham, Anderson, Probst & White conducted the cleaning and renovation of the building from 1986–91. Beyer Blinder Belle of New York converted the first and second floors into an interior shopping arcade in 1991.

Reid, Murdoch & Company Building (1914)

320 North Clark Street

ARCHITECT: George C. Nimmons

One of the first buildings to face the river in accordance with Burnham's 1909 *Plan of Chicago*, the Reid, Murdoch & Company Building recalls that the river was once a working harbor, with manufacturing and warehousing along its length, in this case a wholesale grocery firm. Sharp-eyed observers will note that there is one fewer bay to the west of the central clock tower facing the river than to the east, a circumstance created by the removal of the westernmost bay when LaSalle Street was widened. The composition—central tower, flanking wings, terminal projecting pavilions—is usually traced to French tradition. The regular frame and expanse of glass points to the Chicago commercial vernacular, while the details of the brick and terra-cotta link the building to the Prairie school. More important than these formal attributes is the manner in which this building presents a large size in a comprehensible scale—a value Nimmons wrote about in the architectural press. For many years used for traffic court and other municipal purposes, the building is now being redeveloped for commercial and office uses.

Chicago River (north bank) between State and Dearborn Streets
ARCHITECTS: Bertrand Goldberg & Associates

Affectionately called "the corncobs," this tightly unified complex includes apartments, restaurants, a bank, bowling alley, garage, marina, nightclub, office building, and theater, realizing Goldberg's vision of a city within a city. The twin towers used a sophisticated concrete cast-in-place construction system as each rose to sixty stories, cantilevering the floor plates away from its central core. In December small white and colored lights trace the scalloped edges of many of the apartments, providing a festive aura for a modern icon. Goldberg had traveled to Germany to study with Mies only to be present at the end of the Bauhaus, and he drew on that training to examine problems without preconceptions throughout his career.

Chicago River (north bank) between Wabash Avenue
and State Street

ARCHITECTS: Office of Mies van der Rohe; C. F. Murphy Associates

The tallest American building of Mies's career (one of the towers at the
Toronto-Dominion Centre is higher) was among his last. The freestanding
fifty-two-story building rises 670 feet from its elevated plaza at the river's
edge, further emphasizing its loftiness. The desire to place the building

on a continuous ground plane prevented it from providing access to a lower level, as do some other buildings along the river. Nonetheless, its placement on the plaza, coupled with the river's bend to the east, permits the building to provide a visual termination to the east-west axis of the main branch of the Chicago River as seen from the lake and the bridges along the intervening length of the river. The gray-tinted glass and black anodized aluminum skin serve to present the building as a dark monolith during the day. At night the building is fully illuminated by the interior lights, creating the appearance of a pillar of light. In the winter the heat generated by the light is captured to warm the interior, while that same air handling at the perimeter is used to remove heat and add cooled air in the summer. These interior qualities are matched by the complicated accommodation of the irregular site, including a rail right-of-way near the river's edge. The success of the solution indicates the skill of Mies's colleagues in his office, as, in the last years of his life, he reviewed more than directed the work of others.

[*64*] **35 East Wacker Drive** (1926)
(Originally the Jewelers Building)
ARCHITECTS: Thielbar & Fugard in association with
Giaver & Dinkelberg

Originally the Jewelers Building (the letters "JB" still appear in many passages of the ornament), 35 East Wacker Drive was something of the swan song in Chicago of the historicism of the early 1920s, that predisposition to apply the vocabularies of past ages to commercial buildings. (The Tribune Tower [67] and the Wrigley Building [66] are Chicago's best known examples of the movement.) In this instance, the architects lavished neo-baroque cornices, brackets, and other ornaments across the terra-cotta surfaces of the twenty-four-story main block and the seventeen-story tower of the building, adding a domed pavilion to the very top of the structure and smaller repetitions of the same form at the corners of the main block.

Originally a remarkable parking garage took up twenty-two stories of the interior of the building. Elevators carried cars (without drivers) to

their designated floors and mechanically deposited the vehicles. Inventive though it was, the scheme proved impractical, and it was abandoned in 1940. The floors were then filled in for offices.

[*65*] **Seventeenth Church of Christ, Scientist** (1968)

Heald Square, 55 East Wacker Drive at North Wabash Avenue
ARCHITECTS: Harry Weese Associates

The Christian Science Church has often used strong architectural forms to invite passersby into its facilities. Harry Weese took a prominent site

between the Loop and the river, making a relatively small and low building into a monumental structure on its acutely angled site. The suggestion of a regular, circular, domed form amid the jumble of its surroundings calls attention to its bright travertine-clad surfaces. The transparent glass at grade serves to invite the public in, and clearly visible stair and auditorium forms reveal the interior path to be taken. The sanctuary is most dramatic when the natural light entering from above is heightened in the slanting rays of late afternoon.

Michigan Avenue Bridge Group *(entries 66–69)*

Michigan Avenue Bridge (1920)
Michigan Avenue and the Chicago River
ARCHITECT: Edward H. Bennett
ENGINEER: Hugh Young
SCULPTORS: north end, James E. Fraser; south end, Henry Hering
Equitable Building (1965)
401 North Michigan Avenue
ARCHITECTS: Skidmore, Owings & Merrill; Alfred Shaw &
Associates

Crossing the three branches of the sluggish, reverse-flowing Chicago River has been the subject of intense concern throughout the city's history. With the development of the double-leaf trunnion bascule bridge, all but one of the movable bridges built over the city's waterways since 1903 have been of this type. It combines advantages for both land and water traffic in its quickness and ease of operation. The most impressive of these bridges is at the intersection of Michigan Avenue and the main branch of the Chicago River. Built between 1918 and 1920, it linked Michigan Avenue facing Grant Park to the commercially growing extension of the avenue north to Oak Street and Lake Michigan. A collaboration of the architect Edward H. Bennett and the engineer Hugh Young, the double-decked bridge allows traffic to serve both the upper and lower levels of the avenue and provides efficient service access on the lower level to Wacker Drive, which parallels the river.

When the bridge was sited, the angle of the roads it connected created opportunities for axial exploitation at its northwest and southeast corners, and visual drama at the other two corners. Four of the five buildings that frame this great urban space—most of which is given over to the roadway of the bridge and the river below—were built within the decade following the completion of the bridge. However, while three use

Bedford limestone and one is sheathed in white glazed terra-cotta, each creates or recalls a different architectural source. Once again, the buildings share a general massing—blocks surmounted by distinct towers—and an idea of the nature of the ensemble in which each has a role to play, in which none is subservient. At night the brilliant illumination of the Wrigley Building serves to relate Michigan Avenue facing Grant Park with the extension of Michigan Avenue north of the bridge.

[**66**] **Wrigley Building** (1921, 1924)

400–410 North Michigan Avenue

ARCHITECTS: Graham, Anderson, Probst & White

The first and most prominent of the buildings around the bridge, the Wrigley Building is a prime asset of a consumer products company that understands the importance of a strong, positive image. The building has been floodlit like a billboard from the beginning. The subtly graded terra-cotta gets lighter as it climbs the building. The building's massing descends from the analogy of base, shaft, and capital of the classical orders with the composition of tall buildings. Its ornament derives from Spanish Renaissance sources, while its tower was modeled on the Geralda Tower

in Seville. The 1921 building, close to the river, was so successful that the larger unit and intermediate courtyard were developed by 1924. Automobile access from upper Michigan Avenue and service access from the array of streets below demonstrated Burnham's recommendation, in his 1909 *Plan of Chicago*, for double-decking and separating access to buildings along the river.

Louis Solomon and John Cordwell redesigned the plaza in 1957. Powell/Kleinschmidt restored the lobby in 1984. The building exterior has never been restored. Instead it has received a continuous program of maintenance, including the cleaning, pointing, repair, and when necessary replacement of the terra-cotta.

[*67*] **Tribune Tower** (1925)

435 North Michigan Avenue

ARCHITECTS: Howells & Hood; restoration, Office of John Vinci (1991)

Few buildings in Chicago are more famous than the Tribune Tower, partly because it houses the city's most important newspaper, and perhaps even more because the *Tribune* sponsored a historic international competition, still discussed in textbooks, that attracted some of the world's most famous architects. The building's fame is not without irony. The top prize was awarded to a New York firm, which carried out its design in a manner often thought of as antithetical to "Chicago style" building. Since it is an undisguised application of Gothic style to a skyscraper form, it was regarded almost with contempt during the post–World War II salad days of so-called modernist functionalism. (The "flying buttresses" are cosmetic; they support nothing, a perceived sin against both structural and functionalist faiths.) Moreover, the second-prize entry, by the Finn Eliel Saarinen, is still commonly regarded as one of the most influential unbuilt buildings of the century.

Yet during the past several decades, the Tribune Tower has begun to look better and better to more and more people. The stylistic uses of the past are now more highly regarded, and the tower's image has profited from the shift in taste. And it has gained further by its proximity to the

Wrigley Building (66)—even more beloved, for much the same reason—not to mention by its commanding place in the splendid complex of buildings that surround the Michigan Avenue Bridge.

Much of the building's interior was restored by John Vinci in 1991. The auxiliary but separate building to the east, designed by Jarvis Hunt, was covered with new stone cladding in 1965.

333 North Michigan Avenue (1928)

ARCHITECTS: Holabird & Root

This is the last of the four masonry sky-scrapers that give form to the great urban space around the Michigan Avenue Bridge. Holabird & Root seamlessly blended two models of the tall building on this narrow north-south site. A slim thirty-five-story tower marks the north end with elegant and restrained Art Deco massing, setbacks, and ornament. Fred Torrey made the low-relief carvings of moments associated with the site's history at the transition between the marble cladding of the base and the limestone of the floors above. The telescoping mass-ing at the top of the tower demonstrates the admiration for Eliel Saarinen's several solutions for the tall building dating from his competition entries for the National Assembly in Helsinki in 1908 and the *Chicago Tribune* in 1922. The long twenty-four-story southern section is a thin slab, similar to such early tall Chicago build-ings as the Monadnock. Together, they achieve the transition between the section of Michigan Avenue over-looking Grant Park and the then-new extension of the avenue north to Oak Street. The chamfer at the corners of the tower and the subtle varia-tions between the building's elements along the Michigan Avenue eleva-tion mark the skill of the Holabird & Root firm in achieving their ends. Be-cause of the shift in aligning the prior and new sections of Michigan Avenue, 333's tower serves as a southern focus for Michigan Avenue seen from Oak Street or the Old Water Tower.

360 North Michigan Avenue (1923)
(Originally the London Guarantee and Accident Building)
ARCHITECT: Alfred S. Alschuler

It is instructive of the gap between the tastes of periods and places that 360 North Michigan, a building traditional in all respects, was built a year after Mies van der Rohe had designed the second of his two famous skyscraper projects for Berlin, both of them prophetic of the eventual international triumph of modernism. That distinction aside, 360 Michigan has one asset that seems unassailable: the manner in which the designer freely acknowledged the trapezoidal lot and even emphasized it by the concavity of the facade, with the fortunate result that the building addresses the Michigan Avenue Bridge with optimal spatial effectiveness. The formal language is classical, from the Corinthian columns flanking the arched entrance and the entablature it supports, upward through the shaft to the giant Corinthian colonnade of the attic stories, surmounted in turn by a balustrade and a crowning domed lantern.

North Michigan Avenue *(entries 70–76)*

During the last seventy years, several planned changes in the character and appearance of North Michigan Avenue have turned that thoroughfare from a sedate residential strip into one of the world's most celebrated public concourses. Prior to World War I, when it was known as Pine Street, it was lined with upscale family homes, and most of the traffic that passed from it into the Loop was obliged to cross the river at Rush Street, a block to the west.

Following the recommendations of the Burnham *Plan of Chicago* to create boulevards to alleviate the growing tangle of traffic throughout the inner area, the city elected to widen Michigan Avenue north of Randolph Street, to build a two-level bascule bridge that would connect Michigan Avenue to Pine Street—with a slight jog in the route—and to call the whole passage Michigan Avenue. The inevitable consequence was the transformation of North Michigan Avenue into an increasingly commercial district. The Drake Hotel at its north end and the Wrigley Building at the south, both completed within months of each other in 1920–21, were the first buildings to suggest that a new identity now belonged to the substantially broadened boulevard. Other large structures followed: the Allerton Hotel at Huron Street, in 1924, and the Tribune Tower across from the Wrigley Building, a year later. By the beginning of the 1930s, the Art Deco manner had made its first appearance on the avenue, in the Medinah Athletic Club (now the Hotel InterContinental) just north of the Tribune Tower, and the now-demolished Michigan Square Building at Ohio Street. This last structure, by Holabird & Root, was distinguished by the exquisite foyer known as Diana Court, perhaps the finest piece of Art Deco architecture ever realized in Chicago.

The Michigan Square Building was one of the major victims along the avenue of the impulse to tear down, which is historically nearly as strong in Chicago as the drive to build. (The charmingly eccentric Italian Court at

Ontario Street, by Robert de Golyer, and the solid old 900 North Michigan Building, by Jarvis Hunt, are but two of the area's other prime casualties.) Both tendencies were reactivated shortly after World War II, when the developer Arthur Rubloff proposed turning North Michigan Avenue, already the city's premier street of shops and restaurants, into what he himself envisioned rather grandly as the "Magnificent Mile."

A plan commissioned in 1947 by Rubloff and designed by Holabird & Root would have included, on each side of the avenue, a row of low-rise buildings with another row behind it, separated by a narrow mall of green. This concept was never realized, but the dream of an ambitiously upgraded Michigan Avenue did materialize in the 1960s, 1970s, and 1980s, largely in response to the socioeconomic decline of the old central business district.

Until the 1950s the Loop had been the multichambered heart of Chicago, its veriest downtown, where business was transacted by day and entertainment enjoyed by night. But the coincidence of the exurban flight of the white middle class with the wave of immigration of nonwhite ethnic groups into the city made the Loop unattractive to those who could best afford to keep it alive. To avoid an economic disaster, that is, to retain or to gain back the white middle class as workers, shoppers, and recreation seekers in the inner city, Chicago's big merchants undertook to turn North Michigan Avenue into a second central business district. Water Tower Place, a mammoth urban shopping mall, was the cornerstone of this enterprise. Often likened in habitual Chicago hyperbole to Paris's Champs-Elysées, the avenue of the 1970s and 1980s came to be known among local wags as the Caucasian Fields.

At the outset of the twenty-first century, another change is in process. Two more huge malls, neither of them architecturally distinguished, have lately been added to North Michigan Avenue, suggesting that a gigantism of scale has overwhelmed the modest size and measured elegance that once gave the boulevard its special identity. Meanwhile, among the signs that the Loop is enjoying a return to some of its former magnetism—and attracting a round-the-clock crowd—are the development of a theater district near Randolph Street and the transformation of several older buildings into profitable new hotels and student residences. The resuscitation of the State Street mercantile corridor rests further on the hope of new building on Block 37 (a space bordered by Washington, State, Randolph, and Dearborn that was emptied in the 1980s but left that way when recession struck at the turn of the decade).

Nonetheless, if North Michigan Avenue is not as handsome as it once was, it has maintained its pull on the public, which fills it day and night, shopping, sauntering, and communicating easily. Anyone standing next to the Old Water Tower, at Chicago Avenue, would have to agree that recent changes notwithstanding, the area remains one of the liveliest and most compelling urban passages in the United States.

North Michigan Avenue at Chicago Avenue

ARCHITECT: W. W. Boyington

Most Chicago schoolchildren know the Water Tower as one of the few buildings that survived the great fire of 1871. Even so, their recognition and that of their parents rest equally on the Tower's site and its extraordinary appearance. It is located on one of the most prominent places along Michigan Avenue, and it has become only more familiar to the

public since the boulevard developed into a major shopping district in the 1960s. It is, moreover, as striking to the eye as it is, from an architectural standpoint, stylistically naive. All these factors have anointed it with legend, and Chicagoans are content to venerate it as a monument rather than criticize it as art. Indeed, what is less commonly known is its function. It was constructed as a standpipe (138 feet tall) meant to equalize the pressure of water pumped from the Pumping Station, its obvious counterpart, across the boulevard to the east. Boyington, an early Chicago architect, felt justified in giving the Water Tower a Gothic look, in keeping with the fashions of the day.

[*71*] **Museum of Contemporary Art** (1996)
220 East Chicago Avenue
ARCHITECT: Josef Paul Kleihues

The original home of the Museum of Contemporary Art was a modest one-story rehabilitated industrial building on East Ontario Street. Following a major fund-raising campaign initiated in the late 1980s, and further assisted by the decision of the state of Illinois to deed a choice parcel of land a few blocks north, the museum commissioned Josef Paul Kleihues of Berlin to design its present building. The result, seven times the size of the first MCA, is one of the largest museums in the country devoted to the art of the present.

The exterior is rigorously symmetrical. In front, a broad stair leads through two notched wings from the pavement to the main floor, effectively a *piano nobile*. Most of the outer walls are cast aluminum over a limestone-clad base. Windows are large and square. A thin cornice may prompt the viewer to see classical influences at work, although the modernism of the International Style is more obvious and more to the point.

The foyer, which gives on to a view west toward Michigan Avenue and another east toward the lake, is probably the most rewarding passage in the building. The main floor is divided by a wide corridor into two large galleries usually meant for temporary exhibitions, while the permanent collection typically takes up the four barrel-vaulted galleries on the top level. The ground floor contains a variety of ancillary facilities, includ-

ing a library and a pair of auditoriums. The grounds east of the building, distinctly less symmetrical in plan, include a sculpture garden and patio.

Most Chicagoans find the building cold rather than inviting, but note should be taken of the judicious way Kleihues worked it into its surroundings. Flanked on the south by the gray Gothic of the Northwestern University downtown campus and on the north by a row of mostly inconspicuous apartment buildings, it bows to its neighborhood cordially enough to justify the comment of one of the museum's officials that "we did not want to drop a spaceship on that wonderful piece of land."

845 Michigan Avenue, bounded by Pearson Street, Mies van der
Rohe Way, and Chestnut Street

ARCHITECTS: Loebl Schlossman Hackl; Murphy/Jahn; consulting,
Warren Platner Associates

More than a little controversy has attached itself to Water Tower Place,
which has nonetheless proven one of the most successful buildings on
the avenue in attracting customers to its huge shopping mall, one of the

first examples of the genre to go up in the city as opposed to the suburbs. Many critics have deplored the monolithic density of the building mass as it fronts Michigan Avenue, but even they are likely to be dazzled by the treatment of the lobby, where space given over to the stair and adjacent escalator makes for a visual adventure. Once beyond that point, the shopper may find an ascent in the glass-enclosed elevator no less engaging.

The mall consists of an eight-story atrium with five courts, accommodating more than a hundred shops, restaurants, and theaters. The ninth floor is given over to offices, the tenth and eleventh to the mechanical system and health facilities that are part of the services of a high-rise structure that abuts the east side of the mall. That taller portion of the whole building includes the Ritz-Carlton hotel, with its lobby and accompanying restaurants on the twelfth floor, and above the hotel forty floors of luxury condominiums in the seventy-four-story tower.

[*73*] **Fourth Presbyterian Church of Chicago** (1914, 1925, 1995)
126 East Chestnut Street
ARCHITECTS: Ralph Adams Cram (1914); parish house and manse, Howard Van Doren Shaw (1925); addition and renovation, Hammond Beeby Rupert Ainge (1995)

The view from the cloister of this church to the Hancock tower across the street emphasizes the transformation of North Michigan Avenue from its small-scale neighborhood roots in Pine Street. The complex— church, parish hall, minister's manse, and accessible cloister—provides a low-rise oasis among the surrounding towers. Howard Van Doren Shaw, responsible for the parish house and manse built in 1925, created most of this ambience. Ralph Adams Cram, an architect who championed the cultural, social, and political implications of the Gothic, designed the church. Around the turn of the twentieth century, the Gothic was most strongly associated with religious and educational institutions—such as the Gothic-inspired quadrangles at the University of Chicago. The gray, Bedford limestone structure has finely detailed carving over the door. However, the general simplicity of the building at street level combined with the few steps up into the nave, make this an inviting rather than intimidating church. While the more recent tall buildings have reduced the amount of natural light that can enter the sanctuary, the relative darkness of the interior and the stained glass mean that this has always been a dim rather than radiant space. The combination of masonry walls and piers and timber-framed ceiling yields acoustical properties that enhance the music frequently presented here. Hammond Beeby Rupert Ainge completed a fully accessible new addition, overall renovation, and sanctuary restoration in 1995.

[_74_] John Hancock Center (1970)

875 North Michigan Avenue

ARCHITECTS: Skidmore, Owings & Merrill; entrance redesign, Hiltscher Shapiro (1995)

By far the finest and most interesting of Chicago's 1,000-foot-tall buildings, the assertive, muscular John Hancock Center claims attention as
powerfully as the tapering masonry Monadnock.

A 1,127-foot oil derrick with a building inside, the black X-bracing of
the exterior shows the diagonal load transference of its tubular structure,
the idea of Skidmore, Owings & Merrill structural engineer Fazlur Khan.
The taper—which distinguishes it from its other very tall, but rectilinear
cousins, the Sears and Aon buildings—describes the diminished floor
plates necessary for the mixed uses it contains. Shops and other commercial enterprises are in the lower and concourse levels, including the
wildly popular excrescence of the Cheesecake Factory restaurant by Jor-
dan Moser. Several levels of parking garage yield to twenty-nine stories
of office space. Above these are forty-nine stories of apartments. An observatory, radio and television facilities, and a two-story restaurant are at
the top of the building. Views from the observatory show the city at its
most dramatic.

Along with many other landmarks of modern design, the entry plaza
was unsuccessful from the point of view of passersby on the street. The
reorganization of the multilevel entrance and elevator systems in 1995
also occasioned the creation of a curving waterfall and a sunken plaza,
which manage to be people friendly without compromising the stark
clarity of the building.

[**75**] **Palmolive Building** (1929)
(Previously the Playboy Building)
919 North Michigan Avenue
ARCHITECTS: Holabird & Root

The tendency toward the use of setbacks to add variety to the forms of
the profile of the skyscraper was popular during the Art Deco (often
called Art Moderne) period of the late 1920s and early 1930s. The Palmolive Building at 919 North Michigan Avenue is by consensus one of the
best examples in Chicago. Moreover, while the setback is a horizontal
feature, the architects gained a persuasive contrast in their use of a se-

ries of recessed notches that contributed to the building's overall pronounced verticality.

For nearly three decades, the Palmolive dominated its immediate vicinity, and it was uniquely familiar to all of Chicago on account of the 150-foot airplane beacon (named for Charles A. Lindbergh) that rotated at night, casting its beam at regular intervals across the whole of the city's nighttime sky. With the completion in 1970 of the far taller John Hancock Center just to the south, the beacon, whose light would have shone mercilessly through the Hancock's windows, was rendered obsolete and nonfunctional.

The shops, the elevator lobby, and the facade of the ground floor were restored by Skidmore, Owings & Merrill in 1982. The building will be converted to condominiums by Booth Hansen Associates. Completion is anticipated in 2005.

[**76**] **Drake Hotel** (1920)
Michigan Avenue, between Walton and Oak Streets
ARCHITECTS: Marshall & Fox

Marshall & Fox were the ideal architects for a hotel sited where North Michigan Avenue terminated at the lake. Their carefree elegance created an urbane resort. The tan brick H-shaped hotel block rests on a limestone base full of lobbies, dining rooms, function rooms, and shops. The slight slope of the site means that guests, who arrive at grade on Walton Street, have the surprising and enjoyable experience of seeing the long

expanse of the lake beyond Oak Street Beach from an elevated position once they have traversed the principal rooms of the hotel. The changes in level and direction necessary for a visitor to the Drake add to the pleasure of a visit. The sequence of handsome public rooms is well developed and appropriate for their varied uses. Seen from the lakefront park to the north, the Drake is the right-hand anchor of substantial apartment buildings and hotels on East Lake Shore Drive, and the first element in the great scale jump from the Drake to the Palmolive to the Hancock.

~~~~~~~~~~

[*77*] **860–880 Lake Shore Drive Apartments** (1951)

ARCHITECTS: Ludwig Mies van der Rohe; PACE Associates; Holsman, Holsman, Klekamp & Taylor

Among Mies's most influential buildings, these steel and glass apartment towers are compelling for the practical and proportional brilliance of their individual design and for the innovative solution to the challenge of

the site. The elegance of the facades—uniform on all sides of both buildings—derives from the clear expression of the underlying structural steel frame, which is encased in concrete fireproofing and enclosed by steel plate. The subtle subservience of the glass in the curtain wall to the structure is visible closest to the structural steel columns, where the windows are noticeably less wide than the windows in the center of each bay. The revolutionary use of attached I beams stiffens, punctuates, and adds rhythmic light and shade to the facade. By marching across the facade in a regular pattern, these beams resolve the tension between the thicker steel columns and thinner windows next to them.

The buildings have the proportion of three by five structural bays on each side with a regular structural column grid of twenty-one feet on a side. This means sixteen columns are on the perimeter of the building, and only eight columns are within each building. The result is that virtually all services for the building—elevators, fire stairs, and the various distribution systems of the building—are within the three bays at the center defined by the eight columns. The remaining twelve bays all have the potential for clear and open views out of the building to the city and lake.

Erected over an underground-parking garage that covers the site, the two towers are placed perpendicular to one another, with a critical offset along the west side, similar to the plié in ballet. On the west side, the buildings continue and terminate the grid of the city's underlying form, and the implied triangle created on the east, or lake, side opens the building to the stark grandeur of the lake. One visitor, on seeing a thunderstorm over the lake, thanked Mies for inventing the lightning. While much of modern architecture has been criticized for denying the city and ignoring the natural world, here Mies has achieved a powerful counterpoise between the two.

[**78**] **Northwestern University: Chicago Campus**
Bounded by Erie Street, Chicago Avenue, St. Clair Street, and Lake Shore Drive

The downtown campus of Northwestern University is a sprawling affair, made up of dozens of buildings and pavilions connected in one way or another with medicine and law. Some are part of the university's medical

school, others of its law school, still others of Northwestern Memorial Hospital, the American Bar Association, or institutions like the Rehabilitation Institute of Chicago that are affiliated with but not formally part of the university.

Unsurprisingly, such a vast array—built over eight decades, one structure or at most several at a time, reflecting changing fashions and tastes—hardly constitutes an architectural unity. In the 1920s the row of collegiate Gothic buildings along the south side of Chicago Avenue by James Gamble Rogers, and known as the Alexander McKinlock Campus, did reflect something of a master plan. One can still appreciate the harmony of that group most profitably from the open space remaining on the north side of Chicago Avenue (most of that now belonging to the sculpture garden of the Museum of Contemporary Art [71]), or from the walkway bordering Lake Shore Drive. The four buildings of the Rogers group are the Montgomery Ward Memorial Building (1926), fourteen stories with a five-story tower; Wieboldt Hall (1926), eight stories; Levy Mayer Hall and Gary Law Library (1926); and George R. Thorne Hall (1932), an auditorium.

In the decades following World War II, and especially during the last generation, more and more buildings with medical or legal functions have been added to the complex. Worthy of scrutiny among these are four structures executed in a variety of modernist styles. These include a pair of works by Holabird & Root: the Northwestern University School of Law and the American Bar Association Center (1984) at the southwest corner of Superior Street and Lake Shore Drive, which features a series of setbacks on the north and a handsome exterior wall, both best seen from Lake Shore; and the Northwestern University Health Sciences Building and Olson Pavilion (1978), at the southwest corner of Huron and Fairbanks Court, easily recognizable from its well-proportioned panels of brushed beige aluminum. Gene Summers of C. F. Murphy Associates was chief designer of the Rehabilitation Institute of Chicago (1974), its fawn-colored steel curtain wall suggesting lessons learned from Summers's teacher, Mies van der Rohe. The interior was designed by Norman De-Haan. The most exceptional building in the Northwestern complex houses the Prentice Women's Hospital and Chicago Maternity Center at 333 East Superior and the Ida Stone Institute of Psychiatry (1975) at 320

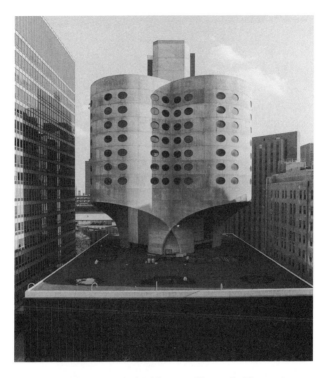

East Huron. Architect Bertrand Goldberg, well known for his use of organically shaped concrete forms, employed that approach here. Atop a four-story rectangular base, a seven-story tower rises, consisting of two intersecting ovals that produce the effect of four cylindrical lobes. This unique structure is supported not by the outer walls or any interior skeleton but by a central core, with the result that floors are free of interior columns. Thus the nursing station at the center of the lobes is efficiently located relative to patients' rooms. Goldberg preserved the curvilinear character of the tower by repeating the shape of the oval in the windows.

The most recent addition to the area is the huge New Northwestern Memorial Hospital (Hellmuth, Obata & Kassabaum, 1999), a suavely designed steel and precast concrete-clad building that evokes the massing of New York's Rockefeller Center. Composed of the Galter Pavilion and the Feinberg Pavilion, it takes up all of the block bordered by Erie Street, Fairbanks Court, Huron Street, and St. Clair Street.

[*79*] **The Arts Club of Chicago** (1997)

201 East Ontario Street

ARCHITECTS: Vinci-Hamp

In one of the bitterest skirmishes in what has lately become something of a full-scale war between preservationists and developers, the Arts Club of Chicago lost out to developer John Buck, who in 1996 oversaw the demolition of the club's storied quarters, the only solely interior space in America designed (in 1951) by Mies van der Rohe. Fortunately, the club had the wherewithal to establish a new home in a building of its own, which it now occupies. At two stories, the buff-colored brick-clad structure enjoys substantially more floor area than the old club. Architect John Vinci's admiration of Mies is clear from his incorporation in the new building of the most dramatic passage of the old club, the serenely geometric stair, its white railings and black carpet framed by the travertine cladding of an elegant surround. A spacious dining room on the top floor and a lounge that doubles as a concert space are the most refreshing parts of Vinci's design. While the Arts Club is a private club, its art gallery on the ground floor, which features a regular series of exhibitions, is open to the public during the club's daytime hours.

505 North Lake Shore Drive

ARCHITECTS: Schipporeit-Heinrich Associates;
Graham, Anderson, Probst & White; associated architects

Among the multitude of high-rise buildings along Chicago's legendary lakefront, none is more arresting than Lake Point Tower. The sinuous curves of the three lobes that make up the shaft are visually fascinating all by themselves, especially as the light plays upon them at various times of day, in assorted weather conditions. At the same time, it is well to remember that the building was conceived with more than aesthetic factors in mind. The contours of the curvilinear plan provided more freedom in laying out individual apartments, while the surfaces of the outer walls made for easier resistance to direct wind loads. At the time Lake Point Tower went up, it was the tallest reinforced concrete building in the world, with a further uniqueness in the form of its flat-slab frame braced by a shear-wall core, triangularly shaped. The landscape at the base of the tower, which includes a swimming pool, ornamental lagoon, and children's play space, was designed by Alfred Caldwell.

[**81**] **Navy Pier** (1916)

600 East Grand Avenue at Lake Michigan

ARCHITECTS: Charles S. Frost (1916); renovation,
Jerome R. Butler Jr., Chicago city architect (1976); renovation,
Benjamin Thompson & Associates and associated architects,
Vickrey, Ovresat & Awsumb (1994)

Grant the newly reconstituted Navy Pier this much: the local architectural profession may hate it, but the public loves it.

Seen from the shoreline, it is a muddle of disparate forms, while up close, its materials look cheap and its detailing careless. Nonetheless, it is a pavilion meant strictly for amusement and recreation, and it provides lots of both. Its claim as the currently most visited attraction in Chicago is borne out by the average number of people—better than 8 million—drawn to it each year.

The 3,000-foot-long pier was built in 1916, one of a pair proposed for the lakefront in Daniel Burnham's *Plan of Chicago* of 1909. Set on twenty thousand timber piles, it was intended originally as a docking and recreational facility, a twin purpose it fulfilled well enough until the 1930s, when shipping traffic on the Great Lakes dwindled. During World War II, it served as a naval training center, and from 1946 to 1965, as the quarters of the Chicago branch of the University of Illinois, later relocated southwest of the Loop (112). During the 1970s and 1980s, the pier fell into disuse except as a venue for occasional special exhibitions. Since a partial restoration in 1976 did little to halt a steady deterioration of the whole structure, the city decided in the early 1990s to carry out a full-scale renovation, which was completed by 1995.

There is admittedly a measure of good sense in the functional order of the plan of the new pier. Closest to the entrance flanked by the old head house is the great variety of shops and amusement and recreational areas that make up the Family Pavilion. This passage gives onto the Crystal Gardens, a two-story space frame housing a children's museum and a botanical garden. Farther to the east is the most visible feature of the new pier, the Ferris Wheel, a giant device echoing the original that dominated the 1893 World's Columbian Exposition. Equipped with forty gondolas, each accommodating six passengers, the Ferris Wheel

rises to a height of 150 feet. The Ferris Wheel and a nearby carousel lead to a huge tented outdoor theater, where popular musical performances take place.

Between that structure and the large groin-vaulted exhibition hall to the east stands the Chicago Shakespeare Theater, erected by Vickrey, Ovresat & Awsumb in 1999 as a separate building. The interior, with seating for 510 persons, is the most architecturally sophisticated new component of Navy Pier. Modeled after the horseshoe-shaped plan of London's Swan Theatre and enlivened by several balconies dressed out attractively in ash balusters, the theater is testimony to the success of the local Shakespeare repertory group.

If the west end is made up mostly of architectural kitsch, the grand old ballroom at the east end remains the most impressive element of the pier. It still conveys the soundly built, intelligently conceived character of the original 1916 pier. The old walkways preserved along the edge of the pier north and south provide a splendid view of the skyline.

Bring the children.

Newberry Library (1893, 1983)

60 West Walton Street

ARCHITECTS: Henry Ives Cobb (1892); addition and restoration, Harry Weese Associates (1983)

Architect Henry Ives Cobb is remembered locally as fluent in a number of the styles popular during the late nineteenth century. He relied on the Gothic mode in the buildings he produced for the University of Chicago (137), but he was equally comfortable in the Richardsonian Romanesque, as his designs for the former home of the Chicago Historical Society (85) and for the Henry C. Durand Art Institute in Lake Forest bear out. The Newberry Library is a variant of the Romanesque, recognizably influenced by the nineteenth-century Boston architect Henry Hobson Richardson in any case.

The library contains one of the nation's outstanding research collections. Plans for the building were meant to follow the instructions of an early librarian who wanted hallways to function almost as separate buildings, thus ensuring quiet in reading rooms on the same floor. The achievement of that objective can be perceived in the two great wings issuing from the central tract of the building.

In 1983 Harry Weese Associates refurbished and restored much of the interior and attached a brick-clad addition to the northwest corner of the building. This new structure, ten stories high (two of them underground), has added stack and storage space to the library. The exterior of the new wing is marked by incised reliefs of round arches on the north and west elevations and by a pair of cylindrical towers at the corners, one for stairs, the other for mechanical risers. Cleaning of the Newberry Library in 1998 revealed the rose color of the granite surface.

[**83**] **Holy Name Cathedral** (1875)
Northeast corner of State and Superior Streets
ARCHITECTS: Patrick Charles Keely; remodeling, Henry J. Schlacks (1914); renovation, C. F. Murphy & Associates (1969)

Designated the cathedral of the diocese when built in 1875, Holy Name is the third church on the site. Initially built in 1846 as the Chapel of the Holy Name of the University of St. Mary of the Lake, it was rebuilt as Holy Name parish in 1854. The 1871 fire destroyed that Gothic Revival brick building. The present building (also Gothic Revival) is constructed of Lemont limestone on a cruciform plan, with central nave and side aisles. In addition to Holy Name, Brooklyn architect Keely also designed St. James and St. Stanislaus Kostka Churches in Chicago. The growth of Chicago occasioned raising the roof with its present water-pegged black walnut ceiling, in 1890–93. Schlacks's work included extending the sanctuary. The five *galeros*, or broad-brimmed red cardinal's hats, of Archbishops Mundelein, Stritch, Meyer, Cody, and Bernardin may be seen suspended high above the sanctuary. Pope John Paul II visited the cathedral during his 1979 visit to Chicago.

[*84*] **Wabash-Huron-Rush-Erie Block**

St. James Cathedral (1857, 1875, 1968)
Southeast corner of Wabash Avenue and Huron Street
ARCHITECTS: tower, Burling & Backus (1857); Edward J. Burling (1875); Cathedral Center, Hammond & Roesch (1968)
Nickerson House (1883)
50 East Erie Street
ARCHITECTS: Burling & Whitehouse
John B. Murphy Memorial (1926)
50 East Erie Street
ARCHITECTS: Marshall & Fox

In the late nineteenth and early twentieth centuries, the neighborhoods along Cass Street (now Wabash Avenue) and Pine Street (now Michigan Avenue) north of the Chicago River were among the favored preserves of the city's social elite. Three notable architectural works from that period still stand on the block bordered by Wabash, Huron, Rush, and Erie.

The parish of St. James, organized in 1834, is the earliest Episcopal parish in Chicago and one of the oldest in Illinois. St. James Cathedral, at Wabash and Huron, became the cathedral of the Episcopal Diocese of

Chicago in 1955, when the original cathedral was destroyed by fire. Part of the present structure, chiefly the tower, dates from the 1857 design, which Burling & Backus conceived in the English Gothic tradition, with a handsome wood-beamed vault commanding the nave. Severely damaged in the Chicago fire of 1871, the church was rebuilt in 1874–75, in a form reportedly faithful to the original. Among the numerous changes made over the ensuing decades, the most important has been the decoration of the interior by the English-born New York architect E. J. Neville Stent, who illuminated the nave, transept, and apse with a myriad of stencils in the Arts and Crafts manner in 1888–89. Stent's treatment was later replaced by other schemes, including that of Thomas Tallmadge in 1925, but the recovery of some of its remaining elements furnished the inspiration for the brilliant restoration of the church by Holabird & Root in

1985. The space is now one of the most coloristically opulent of Chicago's ecclesiastical buildings.

The small St. Andrew's Chapel, located one level below the main sanctuary of the church, was completed in 1913 by Cram, Goodhue & Ferguson after designs by Bertram Goodhue of Boston. It is said to be based on a small abbey chapel in the south of Scotland. To the east is the Parish House by Hammond & Roesch of Chicago, a modernist structure built in 1968 with a clearly articulated and carefully detailed curtain wall. That building is set back from Huron Street, behind a small plaza to the rear of the cathedral. The church intends to destroy the Parish House and put up a condominium tower, now in design.

Adjacent to St. James to the south is the Nickerson House, one of the stateliest and best-preserved relics of Chicago's Gilded Age. The architect, Edward Burling, of Burling & Whitehouse, who also designed St. James, was much sought after by Chicago society of his day. The mansion, built in 1883 with walls of brick some two feet thick, faced with rusticated sandstone on three sides, reflects the style of the Italian High Renaissance. The interior, on the other hand, designed by August Fiedler of Chicago, is a lavish display of stone and woodwork more nearly baroque in character. A special gallery meant to accommodate the Nickerson art collection was also a major feature of the original interior. It was remodeled in 1900 by the Chicago architect George W. Maher for a later owner, Lucius Fisher.

Since 1919 the Nickerson House has been owned by the American College of Surgeons, which uses part of it as administrative offices. The ACS also maintains the impressive auditorium building directly to the east, at 50 East Erie, owned by the John B. Murphy Memorial Association and built in honor of Murphy, a renowned Chicago surgeon. Completed in 1926 after designs by Marshall & Fox of Chicago, the structure bears a striking resemblance to the Chapelle de Notre-Dame-de-Consolation of Paris, erected in 1900 in the grandiose French classical style.

[**85**] **Excalibur** (1892)
(Formerly the Chicago Historical Society Building)
632 North Dearborn Street
ARCHITECT: Henry Ives Cobb

The Chicago Historical Society was formed in 1856, just nineteen years after the incorporation of the city. It established its first permanent home in a building designed by Burling & Whitehouse, which was completed in 1868 and destroyed three years later in the 1871 fire. A second building was finished a generation later, in 1892, after plans of Henry Ives Cobb. The influence of Henry Hobson Richardson, whose name accounts for the term Richardsonian Romanesque, is evident in the use Cobb made here of rough-hewn granite walls, round arched window openings and arcades, and the turrets with conical roofs that frame the main entrance.

The Chicago Historical Society maintained its headquarters in the building until 1931, when it moved to its present site in Lincoln Park (94). An occupant of the structure during and following World War II was the famed Institute of Design, founded in Chicago in 1937 by Laszlo Moholy-Nagy and intended as a revival of Germany's historic Bauhaus, where Moholy taught in the 1920s. The building is now a nightclub.

[*86*] **Medinah Temple** (1912)
Tree Studio (1894, 1912, 1913)
Block bounded by Ontario Street, Wabash Avenue, Ohio Street, and State Street
ARCHITECTS: Medinah Temple, east half of block, Huehl & Schmid (1912); Tree Studio, west half of block, Parfitt Brothers (1894); Hill & Woltersdorf (1912, 1913)

These two buildings seem to share little beyond their adjacency on the same city block. Yet they were both conceived by Lambert and Anna Tree, who recognized that artists need a quiet, serene place in which to work and to display their art. The Tree Studio was principally a place for visual artists to engage in a private search for artistic expression. Residents have included Frances Badger, Ruth Duckworth, Barton Faist, Peter

Falk, Richard Florsheim, Ruth Van Sickle Ford (see the description of her house built by Bruce Goff [168]), Rowena Fry, Oliver Dennett Grover, James Murray Haddow, Charles Hollaway, Jarvis Hunt, Ellen Lanyon, Charles Laughton, Earl Ludgate, Marya Lilien, Hazel Martin (Lady Lavery), Burgess Meredith, John Warner Norton, Pauline Palmer, Albin Polasek, Andrew Rebori, J. Allen St. John, Louis Ritman, Eugene Savage, Rue Carpenter Shaw, and John Storrs. Several of the residents contributed to buildings in this book.

The Medinah Temple had been dedicated to performance, whether, because of its excellent acoustics, for the recordings of the Chicago Symphony Orchestra or recently Disney's *Fantasia 2000*, or in the late winter, as the site for the Shrine Circus. John Philip Sousa, Anna Pavlova, and Luciano Pavarotti have performed there. The sedate profile of the Tree Studio reinforces its purpose, while the exuberant domes, recently restored, and highly textured surfaces of the Medinah Temple promised excitement, the unexpected, and the exotic to its audiences.

Between them they fill their low-rise block with forms that are human in scale and visually diverse, providing an oasis of space and light in the increasingly dense high-rise development that surrounds them. To preserve the buildings, their roles are being transformed. The Medinah Temple has just reopened as Bloomingdale's Home Store, and its acoustics

are now a memory. The Tree Studios are being redeveloped as market-rate apartments with retail uses along State Street. The end of a century-old artists' community—the oldest in the nation, at present—in a complex designed for that purpose is a high price to pay for the preservation of the building designed to achieve that purpose.

[*87*] **Montgomery Ward & Company** (1907, 1974)
Warehouse: 618 West Chicago Avenue
Administration building: 535 West Chicago Avenue
ARCHITECTS: warehouse, Schmidt, Garden & Martin (1907);
administration building, Minoru Yamasaki Associates (1974)

Schmidt, Garden & Martin completed the large warehouse with a concrete frame and brick spandrels in 1907. The impressive unity, clarity, and dignity of such an ordinary building contributed to the interpretation of Chicago building as the source of a modern urban vernacular. This is best seen along the river's edge, where the planar facade bends as the river curves. A strong contrast between the vertical and horizontal can be seen here. The lowest three levels have piers in front of their spandrels, creating a strong vertical rhythm. The upper six floors, by contrast, created an insistent horizontality. Here the brick spandrels extend in front of the concrete piers and were originally unpainted.

The scale of the building evokes the importance of Chicago as a great center for the distribution of goods ordered from the mail-order catalog industry that Ward's pioneered. Currently the building is being re-developed to include aggregated Internet servers—an actual digital warehouse—as well as other commercial, retail, and residential use.

Sheathed in travertine, the Yamasaki-designed administration build-ing appears to ignore the implications of its more humble neighbor. The building is currently being redeveloped as condominiums.

Away from the Core

In American metropolises that took shape during the nineteenth century, the construction of transit lines encouraged citizens to move with gradually increasing speed away from a downtown business district. Thus they were able to retain access to the core while seeking either a residential setting closer to rural nature or a business environment more financially affordable. Although Chicago's growth followed a pattern typical of most American cities, it nonetheless did so in ways peculiar to itself. Its extraordinarily rapid rate of immigration during the late 1800s drove newly arrived inhabitants to cluster in exceptionally dense, unusually tight-knit ethnic settlements. As the earlier subcultures thus established improved their lot, they tended to head toward the city's edges, leaving the less desirable spaces they had abandoned to poorer newcomers. The resultant pattern of sharp contrasts, both ethnic and economic, continues to the present day.

Over the years, the main natural feature that affected the formation of neighborhoods in Chicago was the lakefront. Its continued impact is most obvious today in the ribbon of high-rise apartment buildings along Lake Shore Drive and in the townhouses of Astor Street, both precincts home to the more affluent—even as the city behind them still contains some of the most racially segregated and economically disadvantaged districts in the United States.

The land itself, however, is virtually flat and seemingly endless, of little historic consequence in differentiating one area from another. The river is narrow and easily bridged, once an industrial artery but now more a thoroughfare for boats than a major natural divider. Neighborhoods have been organized less by topographical setting than by human decision, beginning with the federal Ordinance of 1785, which, even before Chicago existed, had foreordained the apportionment of the Northwest Territory into a grid of mile-square sections.

Upon that north-south grid a radial pattern was superimposed, one construct upon another, independent of nature, operating as the chief determinants of Chicago's neighborhood growth. (Among the few exceptions were routes like Clark Street and Ogden Avenue, which followed Indian trails.)

As early as 1869, the city's outward reach facilitated by the rail lines led planners to conceive a system of inland parks connected by boulevards that was meant as a far-flung public urban amenity, punctuating the row upon row of little houses that made up so much of the early inner city. The boulevards followed the grid in a giant C-shaped pattern extending from a point about three miles north of downtown westward about four miles, then southward some ten miles and eastward again about five miles, rejoining the lake roughly seven miles south of the core. Along this route, six large parks ranging from two hundred to six hundred acres each were laid out. Several other boulevards were also part of the 1869 plan, and in the intervening years many smaller parks have been added around the city. The six original greenswards exist today in the form of Lincoln Park and Jackson Park, respectively anchoring the boulevard system at its north and south lakefront connections, and Humboldt, Garfield, Douglas, and Washington Parks, sited along the inland circuit. Similarly, enough of the boulevards remain—for example, Logan, Humboldt, Western, Garfield—that the entire original system may still be perceived.

This immense corporate exercise has done much to animate the tableland of Chicago. Unlike Manhattan, which is focused upon and dominated by Central Park, the Chicago system is decentralized, a fact that further reinforces the identities of the city's neighborhoods. In rather typical Chicago style, the motives behind the scheme stood for a mixture of conflict and cooperation between private interests and public aspiration: developers sought to raise the value of land around the parks and boulevards precisely because those additions enhanced the quality of ambient life. Citizens who could afford to live close to such open space and greenery would thus secure the integrity of their neighborhoods, while the poor living at a distance could reach them by public transportation (presumably without threatening the comfortable neighborhoods). The field houses in those parks functioned as mini–civic centers, providing sports, recreational, and even educational facilities to the people who used them.

Clearly, most of the map of Chicago is still made up of the streets that issue into and out of these parks and boulevards. Here, in the houses that border them, another local tradition is observable. In its earliest decades, Chicago was widely known for its abundance of one-family dwellings, virtually all of them of frame construction. After so many were destroyed in the 1871 fire, apartment buildings often took their place, especially in areas closer to the core. Most of these were two- and three-flat freestanding structures with gabled roofs. Row houses are relatively uncommon in Chicago, where the standard lot width of twenty-five feet—wider than is typical in large eastern American cities—encouraged a degree of sovereign, individualized space that seems in keeping with the city's decentralizing residential tendency. After the city limits expanded greatly around 1890, more and more houses of brick, sometimes with stone facing, appeared. One of the most characteristic forms is the two- or three-flat building, each apartment consisting of a living room lit by a bay window on its front, a dining room, bedrooms and bath in the middle, a kitchen and a porch to the rear, and a small yard and private garage facing the famous Chicago alley, this last device providing an urban delivery and garbage collection system that is among the best in

America. To this house type—the product mostly of the 1900s and 1910s in such inner districts as Lakeview, West Town, and Bridgeport—were added thousands of brick bungalows during postwar decades, the 1920s and the 1950s, in outlying areas like Norwood Park, Austin, Berwyn, and Morgan Park. Commonplace in South Shore and Edgewater is the courtyard apartment building, a form whose appearance in Oak Park and Evanston as well is an indication that the formal boundaries of Chicago often do little to distinguish suburban from adjacent city spaces.

Further to the strength and identity of individual residential neighborhoods were the shopping centers that grew up around the junctions of major streets (e.g., Lincoln and Belmont, Cicero and Madison, and Seventy-ninth and Stony Island). These clusters, where they have survived at all, have lost their former vitality to the ubiquitous shopping malls within and without the city, leaving Chicago neighborhoods to rely for much of their remaining coherence on such institutions as the parish church, the elementary school, and the neighborhood tavern, each cultivating as surely as catering to its own constituency. The frequent siting of the church, for example, Holy Family (114), on a main thoroughfare tends to heighten the public presence of the parish, while elementary schools, like Grover Cleveland (107), have often favored a side-street location, the better to keep children away from heavy traffic and closer to home. The corner bar has traditionally occupied the ground floor of a modest but freestanding apartment building.

However steady some of these patterns may be, change is a historical constant. Even before the turn of the twentieth century, Germans and Scandinavians had moved north and northwest from earlier neighborhoods closer in. Their places were taken up first by Poles, later by Hispanics. Old Jewish settlements on the West Side gradually became African American during the 1950s and 1960s. Pilsen (117), which took its name from a Bohemian population that later moved on to Berwyn and Cicero, has in the past generation turned into a mostly Mexican American neighborhood. Similar scenarios have been acted out in other parts of town by other ethnic groups, not least among them Southeast Asians, lately gathered on or near Devon Avenue. Several waves of immigration in the twentieth century, notably those that carried African Americans north after World War I and Hispanics to the United States as a whole after World War II, have accelerated the moving about, altering the identities of ethnic groups associated with churches and schools (and taverns, too). Moreover, neighborhood cultural centers have lately appeared whose mission it is to strengthen the bond of the people they serve. Largely concurrent with these shifts are recent efforts at gentrification, which have led to the takeover of older districts (e. g., Printers Row, the North Clybourn corridor) by younger professionals or to a historically rare intermingling of those newcomers with established ethnic groups (as in Wicker Park, Bucktown, and Ukrainian Village). Even altogether new neighborhoods have sprung up, like the constellations south of the Loop, some of them, Dearborn Park for one, having risen on abandoned railroad yards. Here and there, areas mostly financed by private interests lie directly contiguous to the city's more forlorn stretches; thus racial and class tensions vie with the hope that the new developments and rehabilitated old ones will help to attract Chicago's lost populations back to the inner city.

Nothing meanwhile has had more of an effect on the fabric of the city than the automobile, which gave rise to the expressways of the 1950s and 1960s and divided neighborhoods physically, sometimes even spiritually, in the process hastening the flight of the middle class to the suburbs.

The negative impact of many of these latter-day changes on the city's services cannot be overlooked in any discussion of Chicago's current urban condition. Only with reliable improvements in education, public transportation, and law enforcement is it likely that substantial neighborhood growth and revitalization will occur.

In that very regard, the past decade has witnessed signs of an upturn in the city's economic fortunes. Families that migrated to the suburbs in search of better schools have watched their children grow up and leave home, thus prompting some parents to return to the city and its urban attractions. In turn, the children themselves have already taken up residence in Chicago; moreover, as they marry and have offspring of their own, some are lately more inclined to stay, impressed by a program begun in the mid-1990s that has as its mission the upgrading of standards in the public schools. In addition, at the turn of the new century, the mayor's office was busy pursuing an assortment of programs aimed at improving the physical look of neighborhoods throughout the city. For the first time in decades, according to the census of 2000, the population of the city proper had increased.

Nevertheless, problems persist, some of them in the form of mixed signals. The literal and metaphoric bloodletting, attributable to gang activity, underscores the need for improved social conditions in the city's long-segregated, long-neglected communities. And many younger families, persuaded that such a locale is not for them regardless of the traffic returning to Chicago, continue to follow the escape route to the suburbs.

Meanwhile, the vastness that stretches away from the core has made room for industry and commerce as well as for areas made up mostly of residences. Chicago's historic commercial prowess derived to a measurable degree from the port facilities situated at its southern edge, while its rail lines enabled manufacturers and entrepreneurs to establish themselves on land sufficiently removed from the center to be cheap yet close enough to attract workers. The city's first industrial park, the Central Manufacturing District, was established by 1900 along Pershing Road near the old stockyards. And the rails were integral to one of the most important architectural accomplishments of Chicago during its 1880–1900 golden age, the town of Pullman, which took shape about fifteen miles southeast of downtown. There, following Chicago tradition, a private citizen, the railroad car manufacturer George Pullman, commissioned a young New York architect, Solon S. Beman, to conceive and assemble a complete planned community, much of which still stands (139).

Yet with the massive shift of recent years that has largely transformed America from an industrial to a service economy, fewer manufacturing plants have gone up either in or outside the city, while entertainment and tourism have grown into industries of a different but significant kind. Chicago now boasts an unprecedented number of first-class restaurants. It has also established itself as a major center of legitimate theater. In the ten years since the last edition of this book, two of its ancient sports arenas have been taken down and replaced— Comiskey Park by a new structure, U.S. Cellular Field, and the Chicago Stadium by the United Center. In turn, Soldier Field is undergoing major changes meant to make it more attractive to larger crowds, especially to corporate patrons who prefer to take in the action from the richly equipped, well-protected spaces called skyboxes. Those alterations have met with considerable opposition, not only from preservationist groups but from observers who believe—with more than a little justification—that the new grandstand is a grotesquely overpowering addition. Only Wrigley Field remains pretty much as it has been in the past, and that is traceable to its special reputation as "the friendly confines," a ballpark whose historic character exceeds in magnetism the competitive record of the team (the Chicago Cubs) that plays there. Add to all this the increased funds the city has poured into enlarging its convention center, McCormick Place, and it should be readily apparent to any observer that the recent change in Chicago's economic identity is reflected in the function of the architecture attendant to it.

Parks and Boulevards

Chicago's parks are divided into three parts: the lakefront park extending nearly the entire length of the eastern edge of the city along Lake Michigan, the system of regional parks and boulevards within the city limits, and the system of forest preserve lands along tributaries of the Illinois River from the Des Plaines west to the Fox. Because the river was always recognized as the best harbor for the area and because the lakefront was originally federal land (Fort Dearborn was here, for instance), it was possible to envision a lakefront park early on. That vision has taken more than a century, but now nears realization.

Likewise, Paul Cornell, an early developer and resident of Hyde Park, proposed the idea of regional parks and boulevards. Between 1869 and 1871, Olmsted & Vaux prepared plans for what are now Jackson and Washington Parks, linked by the Midway Plaisance. After these plans were destroyed in the 1871 fire, H. W. S. Cleveland developed the parks. By the time of Burnham's 1909 *Plan of Chicago*, several other regional parks had been identified and connected by boulevards. The system is nearly complete from Jackson Park on the southeast around a clockwise

arc to Logan Boulevard on the northwest. Only the link from Logan and Western toward the lake is substantially incomplete. A recent identity program has resulted in a series of bracketed signs along the boulevards declaring their history. A second arc of such boulevards was proposed as early as the Burnham plan but has never been realized.

Finally, the forest preserve was established soon after the Burnham plan, and lands for them now create a series of north-to-south linear parklands as far west as the Fox River.

Because the Chicago Park system included a series of field houses, whose programming paralleled that of the settlement house, the parks have an unusually large amount of significant park buildings, in addition to the quality of their overall landscape design. Work by Olmsted & Vaux, Ossian Simonds, H. W. S. Cleveland, Jens Jensen, Alfred Caldwell, and others can be found there, with buildings by William Le Baron Jenney, Schmidt, Garden & Martin, Burnham & Company, Andrew Rebori, Daniel Wheeler, Ralph Johnson, William Carbys Zimmerman, and others among them.

Grant Park, the city's front yard, is in a new phase of transformation through the elimination of railway space, construction of underground parking, and treatment of the park level in a variety of modes. The area named Millennium Park, at the northwest corner of the park, will have open space planned by Skidmore, Owings & Merrill, a monumental sculpture by Anish Kapoor, a music and dance theater by Hammond Beeby Rupert Ainge, and an open-air concert facility by Frank Gehry.

In regional and neighborhood parks, buildings are being rehabilitated, restored, and adaptively reused. A former stable designed by Burnham & Root in Humboldt Park will soon reopen as a Latin American museum and cultural center. Other recent innovative examples include the new Ping Tom Park along the south branch of the Chicago River in Chinatown, and the wetlands restoration in Gompers Park on the northwest side.

[**88**] **Fortnightly of Chicago** (1892)
(Originally the Bryan Lathrop House)
120 East Bellevue Street
ARCHITECTS: McKim, Mead & White

One of the few buildings in Chicago designed by the distinguished New York firm of McKim, Mead & White, the Fortnightly is specially noteworthy for graceful motifs patterned after English Georgian architecture of the eighteenth century. The cornice, the stringcourses, the capstones over the windows, and the shallow relieving arches in the central tract of the first floor testify to the classical origins of the Georgian manner. Curved bays at the ends frame the elegant street facade. Balconies once hung from the three central windows on the second story and the elongated window a floor above. The last of these, as well as the asymmetrical entry, provides a note uncharacteristic of the Georgian. Now serving as the quarters of a women's club, the building was restored in 1972 by Perkins & Will.

North Astor Street between East Division Street and
East North Avenue

Excepting passages of East Lake Shore Drive, Astor Street (named for the
financier John Jacob Astor) has long qualified as the most socially exclu-
sive street in Chicago. It traces its special rank to the construction in
1882, a block to the east, of a grandiose residence designed by Henry
Ives Cobb and Charles Frost for the wealthy merchant Potter Palmer. Located on Lake Shore Drive between Banks and Schiller Streets, the
Palmer mansion, once completed, caused the price of adjacent land to
skyrocket, and presently Astor Street became as chic an address as
Prairie Avenue on the Near South Side had been earlier. The Potter
Palmer house was demolished in 1950, but the area around it has retained its relative value until the present day.

Some sense of the tone of the street is perceptible in the oldest
house still standing, which commands a spacious plot facing Lincoln
Park across North Avenue. Designed in 1880 in a free Queen Anne mode
by Alfred F. Pashley, it was meant as the residence of the Roman Catholic
archbishop of Chicago, which it remains today.

One block south, at Burton, stands the largest house on Astor Street,
an impressive product of the combined efforts of two gifted architects of

different generations: Stanford White of New York and David Adler of Chicago. In 1892 the publisher of the *Chicago Tribune*, Joseph Medill, commissioned White to design the building as a wedding gift for Medill's daughter when she married Robert W. Patterson (who went on to succeed Medill as head of the newspaper). Adler's addition, nearly as large as White's and done at the behest of a later owner of the house, Cyrus McCormick II, occupies the north end of the structure. It follows White's Renaissance Revival model so faithfully that the two components are difficult to tell apart. The building is now a residential condominium.

Comparable in independence of siting if not in size is the James Charnley House at 1365 Astor (90), now known as the Charnley-Persky House. The exterior is unique, due largely to the stylistic originality brought to bear by its designers, Adler & Sullivan (with young Frank Lloyd Wright probably playing some role, since at the time he was in their office). Older and newer buildings along the street, united less by period manner than by individual excellence, but enough of that to ensure an overall cohesiveness, include the neo-Elizabethan James Houghteling houses at 1308–12 Astor, designed by John Wellborn Root in 1887; the Georgian Revival William O. Goodman House (Astor Court) at 1355, designed by Howard Van Doren Shaw in 1914; the French Renaissance Revival Joseph T. Ryerson Jr. House at 1406, designed by David Adler in 1922; and the modernist house at 1524, designed in 1968 by I. W. Colburn. The Art Deco manner is handsomely represented: the Edward P. Russell House at 1444 Astor, designed by Holabird & Root in 1929, and two apartment buildings at 1301 and 1260, designed by Philip B. Maher in 1932 and 1931, respectively.

The first apartment buildings on Astor Street were the McConnell Apartments at 1210, designed by Holabird & Roche in 1897 and marked by some of the same attributes common to that firm's better-known commercial work of the same period. With the 1950s and the increase of high-rise buildings along Astor, it became apparent that height substituting for size and style did more than a little violence to the scale and quality of the neighborhood. The degree of elegance apparent in Bertrand Goldberg's Astor Tower of 1963, at 1300 Astor, is a happy though rare exception.

1365 North Astor Street
ARCHITECTS: Adler & Sullivan

Although Frank Lloyd Wright contributed to this design by Adler & Sullivan, documentary evidence and analysis of the design and plan demonstrate the central role of Sullivan. Regardless of the pride of place in this collaboration, this is among the finest city dwellings in Chicago, occupying a challenging site with assurance and taking full advantage of its position at a jog in Astor Street as it intersects Schiller Street. Orange Roman brick and finely cut limestone are the chief materials of the exterior. The interplay of the severe block of the ground floor and the wooden second-floor balcony contributes to the building's quality. The entry vestibule leads up a few steps to a cross hall and the seemingly vertiginous staircase. The building was restored in the late 1980s by John Eifler of Skidmore, Owings & Merrill. The Seymour H. Persky Fund gave the Charnley House to the Society of Architectural Historians for its use as their national headquarters in 1995.

1328 North State Parkway
Fisher Studio Houses (1937)
1209 North State Parkway
ARCHITECT: Andrew N. Rebori

Post–World War II modernism, notable for ornament-free abstraction, had a stylistic forebear in the Art Deco (sometimes called Art Moderne) that flourished in the late 1920s and the 1930s. The tendency of the earlier movement to streamline form and simplify decorative motifs is expressed with admirable reticence in these two small buildings. The rhythmic repetition of vertical and horizontal lineaments together with the use of glass block (a new material at the turn of the 1930s) are further attributes of Art Deco, and Rebori employs them here with his customary mastery of proportion. The terra-cotta plaques at the Fisher Houses are by Edgar Miller.

[**92**] **Graham Foundation for Advanced Studies in the Fine Arts** (1902)

(Originally the Madlener House)

4 West Burton Place

ARCHITECTS: Richard E. Schmidt and Hugh Garden

In a neighborhood (North State Parkway, North Dearborn Parkway, and North Astor Street) notable for handsome older residences, the Madlener House (now the Graham Foundation) is distinguished by its powerful cubical form and masterly fenestration. Similarities with the Prairie style popularized by Frank Lloyd Wright can be detected in the horizontal detailing of the base, the declarative stringcourses, and the careful grouping of windows. The entrance ornament seems to derive from Louis Sullivan, although Schmidt's assistant and, in this case collaborator, Hugh Garden, referred to it as "Gardenesque." The opulence of the interior millwork was preserved and enhanced in the expert remodeling and restoration carried out in 1963 by the firm Brenner, Danforth & Rockwell. Architect John Vinci recently organized a small yard on the west side of the structure into a garden featuring a fascinating collection of fragments retrieved from demolished Chicago buildings.

ARCHITECTS: Marshall & Fox

Benjamin Marshall and Charles E. Fox, who practiced together from 1905 to 1926, command a unique and unsurpassed reputation for suavely elegant work executed in a manner consistently remote from the modernist revolution. (Among their best known works are the Blackstone Hotel [1910], the apartment building at 999 North Lake Shore Drive [1912], the Edgewater Beach Hotel [1916; unfortunately demolished in 1969], the South Shore Country Club [1916; 138], the Drake Hotel [1920; 76], and the John B. Murphy Memorial [1926; 84]). The apartment building at 1550

North State Parkway is one of the firm's most patently luxurious efforts, its very address widely recognized by Chicagoans and associated with richness of effect. The building, which is clearly indebted to the Beaux-Arts aesthetic, originally featured a single high-ceilinged fifteen-room apartment on each floor, with a central *petit salon* flanked on one side by a *grand salon* with a round bay and on the other by a dining room and orangery. These principal rooms, facing Lincoln Park, comprised a series of formal spaces more than a hundred feet long. On the east side, the bedrooms overlooked the lake, while kitchen, service, and servants' quarters shared the southwest corner of the plan.

[**94**] **Chicago Historical Society** (1931, 1971, 1988)
North Clark Street at West North Avenue
ARCHITECTS: Graham, Anderson, Probst & White; additions, Alfred Shaw & Associates (1971); Holabird & Root (1988)

In its third incarnation, the Chicago Historical Society (see 85) consisted originally of a redbrick Georgian Revival building that had the southwest corner of Lincoln Park to itself. In 1971 the first of two large additions was attached along the full length of the old west elevation. It was widely criticized for its heavy-handed mixture of modernism and classicism, and in 1988 it was replaced, or more exactly encased, by a larger and longer tract. This last addition, now called the Daniel F. and Ada L. Rice Pavilion,

contains the main entrance to the building, on the Clark Street side. While it is intrinsically superior to the first addition in its lively juxtaposition of a redbrick facade with a high-tech frontispiece and a two-story-high curved glass wall at the south end, it is nearly as stylistically unrelated to the old Georgian building as its predecessor was.

[*95*] **Old Town Triangle District**
Bounded roughly by North Avenue, Lincoln Park, and the extension of Ogden Avenue north to Armitage Avenue

The working-class German immigrants who settled the city's Near North Side in the 1850s built frame houses that came to be known as Chicago cottages. The earliest such structures are mostly gone, but those put up in their place retain important similarities. Moreover, they represent a structural innovation achieved for the first time in Chicago, in the 1830s. The so-called Chicago cottage was built using a balloon frame, a construction that replaced the traditional frame in which heavy timber posts and beams, fashioned by hand, had been connected by mortise-and-tenon joints. Since the balloon frame utilized machine-cut lumber and commercially produced nails, which marked it as a vernacular outgrowth of the Industrial Revolution, it could be quickly and easily erected by semi-skilled labor, and it greatly accelerated the settlement of the American West.

The Chicago cottage featured a pitched and gabled roof and typically one and a half or two and a half stories. It had a high basement and a raised front entrance next to a grouping of windows. Sometimes decorated, sometimes not, it was a common form of housing until an ordinance passed in 1874—after the great Chicago fire—proscribed frame construction within city limits. In the Old Town neighborhood, row houses followed, customarily of Italianate or Queen Anne style. Five such houses, at 1826–34 North Lincoln Park West, bear the unique hand of Louis Sullivan.

In the late 1940s, the area was the site of one of the nation's first planned neighborhood revitalization projects. Since then, many small but historic houses have been lovingly rehabilitated, leaving Old Town with much of its old charm and, ironically, free of the high-rises that have disturbed the scale of wealthier districts closer to the lake.

[*96*] **Steel and Glass House** (1981)
1949 North Larrabee Street
ARCHITECT'S: Krueck & Olsen

Because it is a private residence, the Steel and Glass House is not open to the public, but the facade facing the street is striking enough to give

the viewer a fair notion of the materials suggested by the name of the house and of the determination of the architects to take optimal advantage of a form they have often called the seminal component of their own expressive vocabulary: the rectangle. The front is a well-proportioned union of three steel-framed bays horizontally articulated, adjacent to two vertically, the latter covered with a steel grating through which a glass block half-cylinder enclosing a spiral stair is visible. The interior is C shaped, its two rectangular arms joined by a two-story living room that opens to an inner court. While the designers acknowledge, and even celebrate, their debt to Mies, the two-story-high living-room area more readily recalls a similar habit of the great Swiss Le Corbusier, while the glass block cylinder is conceived as an homage to Pierre Chareau's 1930 Maison de Verre in Paris.

[*97*] **Mid-North District**

Bounded roughly by Fullerton Avenue, Clark Street, Armitage Avenue, and Lincoln Avenue

This area has changed markedly since the 1870s, when it constituted the northern built-up edge of the city. At that time, spaces between its modest frame houses were wide enough to halt the spread of the Chicago fire of 1871, which finally died out there. In the wake of the mammoth blaze, brick row houses and freestanding dwellings went up, producing a neighborhood of greater density and a perceptibly urban character.

During the last several generations, Mid-North has grown progressively affluent. Professionals have found its scale attractive and its location close enough to downtown that real estate values have steadily risen since World War II. Several individual buildings are noteworthy both historically and architecturally, including a modest trio of structures that survived the fire: the Bellinger Cottage at 2121 North Hudson Street and houses at 2339 and 2343 North Cleveland. Two works by the young Louis Sullivan may be seen at 440 West Belden (1883) and 2147 North Cleveland (1884).

[*98*] **McCormick Row House District** (1882–89)
Between Belden and Fullerton Avenues, Halsted Street, and the elevated tracks
ARCHITECTS: A. M. F. Colton & Sons

The district owes its name to Cyrus McCormick, staunch Presbyterian and inventor of the reaper, whose promise of financial backing led the Indiana Theological Seminary to move to Chicago at the turn of the 1860s,

adopt the name McCormick Theological Seminary, and build a new campus on the city's North Side. The houses that comprise the most memorable parts of the area went up in the 1880s, following traditional styles. The earliest of these, fronting Belden and Fullerton Avenues, are in a simplified Queen Anne style notable for ornamental brickwork and stone trim. Divided from these by a private park bordered by sedate little Chalmers Place is a later row of houses, more severe in character yet agreeably unified. They feature deeply indented entrances and windows crisply cut in brown brick trimmed in brown stone. Round arches appear on several of the facades, while the roofline consists of symmetrically alternating round and triangular gables. In 1975 McCormick Theological Seminary joined the theological schools of the University of Chicago and moved to the University's South Side campus. Thereafter, private citizens acquired the row houses and DePaul University took over the old seminary's institutional buildings.

[**99**] **Elks National Veterans Memorial** (1926)
2750 Lakeview Avenue
ARCHITECTS: main building, Egerton Swartwout; magazine building, Holabird & Root (1967)

Few buildings in Chicago convey the character of a monument more emphatically than this ensemble. The central element is a huge cylinder with a frieze at its upper reaches and, above that, a flattened dome that rises

a hundred feet above the floor. Surrounding this unit is a thirty-eight-foot-high colonnade that rests upon a larger cylinder topped by a belting frieze in high relief. The colonnade supports a powerful cornice from which the dome appears to ascend.

The Memorial is also notable for interior and exterior sculptures by Gerome Brush, Adolph A. Weinman, James Earle Fraser, and Laura Gardin Fraser, as well as a program of murals in the interior, executed by Edwin H. Blashfield and Eugene Savage.

[*100*] **Brewster Apartments** (1893)
2800 North Pine Grove
ARCHITECT: Enoch Hill Turnock

Turnock took advantage of a typical corner site by presenting a monumental, undulating mass to the angled and axial block of Pine Grove to the south. Although the area of the windows of the facades is roughly equivalent to the opaque surface of the stone, the quartzite is rock-cut.

This roughness, emphasized by the rounded corner oriels and polygonal wall bay windows, seems to make the building into a rock outcrop. Despite the massiveness of the exterior expression, the building is arranged around a rectangular light court, a dwelling type of great antiquity. Since this is an elevator building, Turnock used this space for circulation up and down the elevators, and along bridges at every level leading to the individual apartments. Here a light metal frame and glass block flooring create a lattice of line and light that is unexpected, unfamiliar, and uplifting.

[*101*] **Alta Vista Terrace District** (1904)
One-block-long street, running north-south, located at
3800 north and 1050 west
ARCHITECT: J. C. Brompton

Anyone who comes upon this single-block street will immediately recognize its uniqueness within a North Side neighborhood otherwise free of distinguished architecture. Alta Vista is something of a paradox, a se-

quence of masonry row houses each stylistically different from its neighbor yet together somehow comprising a unified whole. To a degree, this identity derives from the uniform two-story heights of the forty houses that occupy lots twenty-four feet wide and just forty feet deep. Twenty such structures rise cheek-by-jowl on each side of a relatively narrow, 480-foot-long street stretching from Byron Street on the north to Grace Street on the south. Brick party walls eighteen inches thick join the houses, which are variously decorated with Doric and Ionic wood pilasters, flamboyant Gothic arches, Palladian windows, stained- and leaded-glass fanlights, bay and bow windows, sheet-metal cornices at roof levels, and a profusion of classical brackets, dentils, festoons, moldings, and other details.

[*102*] **Immaculata High School** (1922)
640 West Irving Park Road
ARCHITECT: Barry Byrne

Byrne studied architecture in Frank Lloyd Wright's Studio from 1902 to 1908 and retained the respect of his mentor throughout his career. He sought to integrate his progressive architectural ideals with progressive

liturgical values in his many religious commissions. Immaculata High School occupies a site just south of Wright's influential, but since destroyed, Husser House. The subsequent construction of Lake Shore Drive and the extension of the lakefront park have cut off the building from its original view overlooking the lake. The brown tapestry brick walls, limestone details, and red tile roof create a subdued fabric for the L-shaped building. The lancet windows of the easternmost element indicate the large gathering spaces within, while the more regular and repeated windows of the westernmost element describe the repetitive classroom spaces they light. Alfonso Iannelli, a sculptor and frequent collaborator with Byrne from their first association in Wright's Studio, created a statue of the Virgin, whose purity is recalled in the school's name, over the principal entrance, in the re-entrant angle. Byrne also designed two additions, a convent in 1955 and a western extension of the school in 1956. The American Islamic College, its current owner, removed the statue, which is now in the collection of the Chicago Historical Society.

[*103*] **Hutchinson Street Landmark District**
Hutchinson Street between Marine Drive and Hazel Street

The uniqueness of this neighborhood is a reflection more of authorship than of styles. Virtually all the houses here were designed late in the nineteenth century and early in the twentieth by George W. Maher, whose customary identification with the Prairie school sometimes does disservice to his ability to work creatively on his own and in more than a single manner. A measure of eclecticism is thus apparent throughout this area. The first of the houses—a lively exercise in Queen Anne sporting a wealth of projecting bays, porches, and turrets—went up in 1894 at the northeast corner of Hutchinson and Hazel Streets.

Nevertheless, the horizontals that dominate the exterior of the house at 826 Hutchinson Street, dated 1904, do provide evidence of the influence of the early work of Frank Lloyd Wright, as does the house put up in 1913 at 817 Hutchinson, arguably the most impressive of Maher's efforts in the neighborhood. With its long bands of windows, it is also regarded as an illustration of Maher's motif-rhythm theory, in which repetition of a

decorative element in a design was seen as crucial to achieving the unity of the final result. The front entrance of Maher's 1902 house at 750 Hutchinson is framed in stone, in a manner further suggestive of stylistic debt, this one to Louis Sullivan's Wainwright Tomb in St. Louis.

Hard upon these works is a building also worthy of mention, by another architect. The carefully detailed residence at 4234 Hazel Street was designed by William Drummond, similarly associated with the Prairie school, who at the time of the completion of the house, 1904, was at work in the office of Richard Schmidt.

[*104*] **Graceland Cemetery** (1860–)

4001 North Clark Street

LANDSCAPE ARCHITECTS: H. W. S. Cleveland,
Ossian C. Simonds

H. W. S. Cleveland's early plan for the cemetery, dating from the 1860s, was later revised and enlarged by Ossian Simonds. Paths and roadways are laid out in the informal, curvilinear manner true to the mid-nineteenth-century romantic vision of the cemetery as a picturesque nature-bound retreat rather than the traditional tightly composed churchyard. The largest plots, serving the most renowned of the deceased, are grouped around an artificial lake, Willowmere, near the northern boundary of the cemetery. In recent years, planting patterns based on nineteenth-century practice have been introduced with varying success.

Since Graceland Cemetery has long been the chosen burial ground of Chicago's elite, it is not surprising that it is of interest to tourists. Other cemeteries in the region of similar quality include Rosehill on the city's North Side, Oak Woods on the South Side, and Forest Home/Waldheim in the near west suburbs. While visitors flock to Graceland to view the graves of people with names like Armour, Field, McCormick, Palmer, and Schoenhofen, the great commercial builders of the city, what they often find are family monuments created by the most illustrious architects of the city. Thus the mastaba-like tomb of Martin Ryerson and the elegantly decorated mausoleum of Carrie Eliza Getty were designed by Louis Sullivan, while George Pullman's remains repose beneath a single lofty Corinthian column by Solon S. Beman.

Some of the architects themselves are memorialized by their colleagues: John Wellborn Root by Charles Atwood and Jules Wegman of D. H. Burnham & Company, Sullivan himself by Thomas Tallmadge and others, Ludwig Mies van der Rohe by his grandson Dirk Lohan. Preservationist Richard Nickel lies in a grave marked by a monument designed by John Vinci. Other architects buried here include Howard Van Doren Shaw, Bruce Goff, and Daniel Burnham, as well as the structural engineer Fazlur

Khan, responsible for the braced and bundled tubes of the Hancock Center and Sears Tower.

Chicago's most famous early-twentieth-century sculptor Lorado Taft is responsible for the figure of Death that guards the tomb of Dexter Graves. Henry Bacon designed the seated reflective female figure that centers the Marshall Field plot.

Among the many other notables buried in Graceland are the boxers Jack Jefferson and Bob Fitzsimmons, baseball magnate William Hulburt (note the baseball-shaped tombstone!), the newspaper publishers Victor Lawson and Joseph Medill, the statesmen Governor John Peter Altgeld and Mayor Carter H. Harrison, and the designer-educator who revived the Bauhaus in Chicago, Laszlo Moholy-Nagy. The body of early Chicago architect William Le Baron Jenney lies in an unmarked grave in the Jenney family plot.

Holabird & Roche designed several buildings, including those at the entry, the crematorium, and the original part of the chapel.

[*105*] **Krause Music Store** (1922)
4611 North Lincoln Avenue
ARCHITECTS: Louis H. Sullivan and William C. Presto

The facade of the former Krause Music Store is Louis Sullivan's last completed building. William C. Presto was an architect of small-scale neighborhood commercial buildings. Presto had enjoyed working briefly for Sullivan on the Columbus, Wisconsin, bank. He invited Sullivan to design the terra-cotta facade for this small music store with apartments above in an area of many German immigrants. The most elaborate element of the richly developed facade, a giant keylike cartouche, ties the first floor to the parapet of the roof. Sullivan's own love of music is well known, and his facade invited entry into the world of music and the treasures of the shop. The delicate ornament framing the large single-paned glass shop window, with its surrounding electric lights, adds to the pleasures of window-shopping in the evening. In certain lights the gray-green terra-cotta has undertones of blue. The shop has had varied uses, and a since-departed gallery restored the shop window.

[**106**] **Carl Schurz High School** (1910)

3601 North Milwaukee Avenue at Addison Street

ARCHITECT: Dwight H. Perkins

Named for the distinguished German American reformer, Carl Schurz High School speaks to the growth of Chicago as an immigrant city. Dwight Perkins composed this very large building as a series of interlocking forms, distinguished by the color and texture of his materials, in-

cluding a tawny stone, purple brick, tan terra-cotta, and red tile roof. The interlocking forms and broad horizontality of the building proclaim its links to the Prairie school. The overlapping of the steep roofs and the interest in color may be derived from contemporary developments in northern Europe. A great lawn, punctuated by locust and Osage orange trees, fronts the building, making it handsomely and comprehensively visible from Milwaukee Avenue. Later wings by other architects followed Perkins's design very well. The 1994 cleaning by Ross Barney & Jankowski reveals the stunning polychromatic richness of the building, hidden under years of grime.

3121 West Byron Street
ARCHITECT: Dwight H. Perkins

The severity of Perkins's design is relieved by several factors. The facade is enlivened by borders made of contrasting brick and by piers whose termination in capital blocks creates a clean transition to the walls above them, thus reinforcing the secure proportioning of the whole composition. The piers recall Gothic buttresses, but they are simple enough to harmonize with the overall abstractness of the surface decor.

Northwest far city limits, junction of Northwest Tollway and Tri-State Tollway
ARCHITECTS: Naess & Murphy; C. F. Murphy Associates; Murphy/Jahn; Perkins & Will; O'Hare Associates; I. M. Pei Associates

Among the world's busiest airports, O'Hare is a mammoth enterprise whose steady growth since it opened in 1963 continues as the new century unfolds. Most phases of design have been supervised by the same Chicago architectural firm, which has meanwhile changed its name from

Naess & Murphy to C. F. Murphy Associates and now to Murphy/Jahn. The latest completed major building at the airport, the International Terminal, is the work of another large local office, Perkins & Will. The original control tower is based upon a prototype, designed by I. M. Pei Associates (1972), that can be found in a number of American airports. A new control tower meant for the United Terminal was added later by Murphy/Jahn.

The chief designer of the earliest terminals at O'Hare (now called 2 and 3), together with their attached concourses, and of the heating and air-conditioning plant as well as various service buildings, was Stanislav Gladych. Gertrude Kerbis was principally responsible for the restaurant that connects terminals 2 and 3. Recognizably Miesian in their lean, rectilinear steel-and-glass geometry, these several structures lent a consistency of appearance to the early O'Hare that continued with the addition of the O'Hare Hotel (now the Hilton, chief designer John Novack) to the complex in 1972.

With the completion, also in 1972, of an immense 9,000-car parking garage (chief designer Gladych), O'Hare reached the end of its first phase, whereupon the taste of a new generation became manifest. In

basic form, Terminal 1, designed by Helmut Jahn and occupied by United Airlines, retains the Chicago tradition of the expressive use of the frame structure, most obvious in the folded roof trusses of the pavilion and the vaults that cover the lofty parallel Concourses B and C. Otherwise, the new building departs the Miesian model in favor of a more patently technological vocabulary, as animated as it is aggressive.

Color, assigned an important role in Terminal 1, is most noticeable underground, where Concourses B and C are connected by a moving walkway. The most visually fascinating components of this 800-foot long tunnel are the variegated undulating glass walls and the overhead neon sculpture by Michael Hayden.

The feeling for color in Jahn's work at O'Hare has been carried further in the decorative nuances that marked the remodeling of Gladych's older concourses in Terminals 2 and 3, and especially in another underground passage of the complex. This last is the final stop, the O'Hare station, on the public transit rail line that runs on the median strip of the John F. Kennedy Expressway connecting the airport directly with downtown Chicago. The most notable feature of the station, designed by Jahn in 1984, is a tall wall of backlit, gold-illuminated glass block flanking the tracks. It is articulated in a vertical rhythm of alternating ridges and grooves akin to the treatment of the walls of the aforementioned connecting tunnel at Terminal 1.

One of the largest and most ambitious of the O'Hare buildings is Terminal 5, the International Terminal, designed chiefly by Ralph Johnson of Perkins & Will and opened in 1993. Chicago's position as a major connecting point in global travel necessitated not only this project but its formidable interior, measuring 1 million square feet. Its location adjacent to the principal entrance route to O'Hare, and in front, or east, of the main mass of buildings, makes it the first airport structure visible to motorists arriving from the city, as well as to travelers coming from abroad.

The building is composed of three levels, with the lower two given over to arrival facilities, baggage handling, and related services. The top level is a generously proportioned, boldly structured departure hall, a veritable galleria, whose curvilinear roof admits an ample quantity of natural light. The plan is roughly crescent-shaped, with concourses arranged along the outer curved edge and extended outward from the terminal in two great arms.

The various facilities at O'Hare have expanded over so large an area that an automated rail transit system has been installed by O'Hare Associates with Murphy/Jahn, chiefly to move passengers between the new International Terminal and the older terminals, the main parking garage, and the remote parking lots.

Another chapter in the history of the airport's architecture commenced early in 2001, and since completion is expected as late as 2007, this phase, the third, gives the appearance of being substantial in its impact. Terminals 2 and 3 will be subjected to considerable change and expansion. Canopies will be extended from the front of the two units to cover an expanded and functionally more efficient sidewalk area as well as a portion of the roadway. Interior volumes will also be increased, with walls, floors, ceilings, and illumination taking on a new high-tech look. Other changes will affect the security stations, the baggage claim areas, and internal passageways. The addition of elevators and the reorganization of escalators will aid pedestrian movement. At the beginning of the third phase, alterations were also envisioned for the facades of all three domestic terminals, but the effect on the airlines of the September 11,

2001, attacks has resulted in budgetary cutbacks. Thus, the facades of only Terminals 2 and 3 will be redesigned, though in an integrated manner following Helmut Jahn's sleekly handsome treatment of steel and glass. The ultimate goal remains a stylistic unity of all three terminals.

[*109*] **St. Mary of the Angels Roman Catholic Church** (1920)
1850 North Hermitage Avenue
ARCHITECTS: Worthmann & Steinbach; restoration, Holabird & Root (1992)

One of the most ambitious of Chicago's many neighborhood churches, St. Mary of the Angels reflects a strong influence from the Roman High Renaissance. Its most compelling external element is a dome, reportedly modeled after the rotunda Michelangelo designed for the basilica of St. Peter in Rome. A five-aisled interior, one of the most capacious among Chicago churches, features a barrel-vaulted nave that meets the transept at the crossing, where the dome, resting on pendentives, rises 135 feet above the floor. Built for Polish immigrants, St. Mary enjoyed its most prosperous years between 1920 and 1950. Later demographic changes have led to a variety of ethnic groups, chiefly Hispanics, as well as urban professionals from Bucktown and Wicker Park, to share the church with its original Polish congregation.

Gradual deterioration of the structure necessitated its closing in 1987, but a program of renovation, supervised by Holabird & Root, has returned to it much of its handsome original condition. The stained-glass windows, many of them designed by the Zettler atelier of Munich, have been restored by Rigalli Studios of Chicago. The church reopened in 1992.

[*110*] **Holy Trinity Russian Orthodox Cathedral** (1903)
1121 North Leavitt Street
ARCHITECT: Louis H. Sullivan

In the midst of a stable working-class community, Holy Trinity demonstrates Sullivan's flexibility in design and continuity of ornament. Although he urged architects to create an organic American architecture in his *Kindergarten Chats*, here he duplicated the organization and form of a typical Russian Orthodox church—towered entrance, ample narthex, centralized sanctuary. The building was budgeted at $27,000, and Czar Nicholas II contributed $4,000. The broad stuccoed surfaces of the exterior brick walls serve to highlight the wooden framing elements with their richly developed surfaces. With incised ornamentation, as in the metal entry hood, the entire building is a formal exploration in two and three dimensions of the relationship between the square and the circle. As its exterior suggests, this modest building contains a richly elegant interior. Holy Trinity was designated a cathedral in 1923.

[*111*] Jackson Boulevard District

1500 blocks of West Jackson Boulevard and West Adams Street,
200 block of South Ashland

In the quarter century that bracketed the Civil War—the period when Chicago and the nation became a major industrial power—the Near

West Side of Chicago was a neighborhood of choice for many of the elite. Centered along Ashland Avenue from Union Park to Taylor Street are still to be found the monumental forms of several important churches. Extending east of Ashland in the middle of this zone, the Jackson Boulevard District contains a very complete set of dwellings representative of the domestic design ideals of the period. Mayor Carter Harrison lived here, as did Benjamin Ferguson, whose commitment to endowing public sculpture continues to enrich the city. Identification of its qualities and efforts to designate the district began in the 1960s, reflecting the national trend of neighborhood preservation. The landmark designation of the district in 1976 has both confirmed the strong cohesion of the district and permitted subsequent maintenance of that quality. The 1997 expansion of this district testifies to the success and popularity of such actions.

[*112*] **University of Illinois at Chicago** (1965–)

Generally bounded by Harrison, Halsted, Taylor, and Morgan Streets
ARCHITECTS: general plan, Skidmore, Owings & Merrill; Walter Netsch design partner; modifications of general plan, Daniel P. Coffey & Associates (1994)

Initially intended as a great public undergraduate university for students who were expected to commute to school, the campus is sited near a series of intersections of major road and rail transportation links. The faculty and students were expected to circulate rather like automobiles, with high-level express walkways and grade-level local walks. At the center of the campus was a complex of lecture halls and open spaces described as an intellectual agora. To pull all this together, Walter Netsch used the geometries of his field theory, which he believed would provide a comprehensive sense of order for the students in the midst of a very large complex. The practical and symbolic merits of this plan were so thoroughly disputed that, in 1994, the raised walkways and central space were removed in an effort to make the campus seem friendlier and more human in scale.

Although the rigors of a deeply modern architectural design have been discarded for the comforts of a familiar campus, the transformation of the campus, its buildings, and its neighborhood clearly reflect the university's evolution from a predominately undergraduate institution to one with a thriving graduate program. New dormitories, likewise, accommodate the shift from an exclusively commuter campus to one with a growing residential component. Current expansion has removed all traces of the fabled Maxwell Street market, where the blues, fried pork chops, and axle grease filled and scented the air.

[**113**] **Jane Addams Hull House and Dining Hall** (1856, 1905)
800 South Halsted Street
ARCHITECTS: house, unknown (1856); dining hall, Pond & Pond (1905); restoration and reconstruction, Frazier, Raftery, Orr & Fairbank (1967)

Jane Addams would not recognize this memorial to her pioneering work in the settlement house movement. The 1967 restoration removed the third floor of Hull House, which Jane Addams had added, and restored the cupola and wrap-around porch, which Addams had removed. Hull's original Italianate house was first built in a suburban setting that was subsequently engulfed by the rapidly growing city. From 1889, when Ad-

dams first began using space in the former house of Charles Hull, until her death in 1935, she and her colleague Ellen Gates Starr continuously expanded and transformed this building. A dozen other buildings, of which the dining hall alone survives, were added to create a large complex designed by Irving and Allen Pond. The Ponds had visited Toynbee Hall in England, as Addams had before them, in order to study the allied purposes of the settlement house and the Arts and Crafts movements. The new campus of the University of Illinois at Chicago required that the other buildings be demolished. Even the dining hall was relocated two hundred yards from its original site. The Hull House Association continues as a social service agency dispersed throughout the city.

[*114*] **Holy Family Church** (1874)
1080 West Roosevelt Road
A R C H I T E C T S : exterior, Dillenburg & Zucher; interior,
John Mills van Osdel; upper steeple, John Paul Huber
St. Ignatius College Prep School (1869, 1874)
1076 West Roosevelt Road
A R C H I T E C T S : Toussaint Menard; addition, John Paul Huber (1874)

Several assets aside from the beauty of Holy Family's interior are worth remarking. Begun in 1857, the church serves Chicago's original Jesuit parish, and the building is the only surviving example of pre–Civil War Gothic church architecture in the city. With a single spire rising 236 feet, it was the tallest Chicago structure until Burnham & Root's Masonic Temple went up downtown in 1892. The chronological order of Holy Family's congregations is a measure of the historical movement of immigrants in Chicago, with the Irish and the Germans giving way later to the Italians, and most recently to Mexicans and African Americans.

The exterior of the church, by Dillenburg & Zucher, is faced with yellow brick and masonry (recently cleaned), while John Mills van Osdel's interior features powerful compound piers that have settled—stably—as much as eighteen inches out of plumb. Especially notable is the program of stained-glass windows, the best installed in 1907 (the church's fiftieth anniversary) by the Von Gerichten Art Glass Company of Columbus, Ohio.

Earlier still, in fact the oldest surviving stained-glass windows in Chicago, are those in the clerestory. They were designed and put in place in 1860, by the W. H. Carse Company of Chicago. Paintings and sculptures abound, with the altar graced by thirteen large and imposing statues, the work of Anthony Boucher, a German immigrant.

A remarkably convincing restoration, carried out during the 1990s, was supervised by Chicago architect John Vinci. Patrick J. Caddle and Leon Kelleher worked on the statuary and Robert Furhoff on the columns and walls.

St. Ignatius College Prep School, to the east, is modeled somewhat naively after the Second Empire style popular in America following the Civil War, but the interior contains some of the most compelling spaces surviving from pre-fire Chicago. The tall ceilings of the foyer and hallways reward the visitor who has reached them by way of an exterior entrance stair. Additions and renovations were carried out by several architects in the 1980s. The most impressive space is the Brunswick Room on the top floor. Designed by an unknown architect in 1888 and recently returned to its original state, it is a balconied library most notable for its carved wood. Elsewhere in the building, many stencils have been restored, while new ones, designed and executed by Robert Furhoff in 1990, now embellish the main working library.

[*115*] **Illinois Regional Library for the Blind and
Physically Handicapped** (1978)
1055 West Roosevelt Road
ARCHITECTS: Stanley Tigerman as consultant to
Jerome R. Butler Jr., city architect

Until 2003 this building housed a state distribution center for Braille library materials as well as a citywide library for the blind and physically
handicapped and a local branch of the Chicago Public Library. Circulation
areas were arranged in linear order and featured built-in furnishings that
were simple to memorize for easy maneuvering.

Directly inside the west wall was the circulation corridor, defined by a
long counter that curved inward at each of four service desks so that a
user could approach it without using the main aisle. The curving corridor
is reflected on the exterior by a whimsical undulating window set into
the concrete wall. The lower part of the window enables someone in a
wheelchair to look inside, while the higher points are opposite the service desks so that library personnel could see out.

The architect intended paradoxes throughout the design. The lightweight baked enamel panels are made to seem heavy, since they are
only infrequently opened by the insertion of small windows. On the other
hand, the structural concrete wall is broken by the undulating window,

which amounts to an incision so long and sustained that the rampart it is part of seems curiously insubstantial. Because the stacks were organized on three levels, the smaller exterior elements are three stories high, and the larger elements are only two stories. At the same time, the structure is brightly colored, with structural parts painted yellow, mechanical ducts and electrical and plumbing conduits blue, the metal wall panels red. It offers a vivid contrast to drab surroundings and enlivens a structure that served a very serious purpose.

[**116**] **Schoenhofen Brewery** (1902)
West Eighteenth Street and Canalport Avenue
ARCHITECTS: Richard E. Schmidt; Hugh Garden

The widespread tendency of architects at the turn of the twentieth century to move away from revivalist and historicist styles toward a more straightforward expression of form is apparent in this recently and faith-

fully restored building. The massing is cubical, with the right angle dominant and decoration derived from an unmannered application of brick. The single deviation from rectilinearity, more agreeable than contradictory, appears in the powerful round arch of the entrance. While Schmidt was the architect-of-record, the design was evidently carried out by Garden, whose assistance Schmidt called upon from time to time in the years prior to their formation of a partnership in 1906. Note the similar relationship of their work on the Madlener House (see Graham Foundation [92]).

[*117*] **Pilsen**

Bounded roughly by West Sixteenth Street, South Halsted Street, West Cermak Road, and South Western Avenue

No area of Chicago contains more material evidence, much of that architectural, of the historical pattern of movement of various ethnic groups into and out of the city's neighborhoods. Pilsen is now home to a His-

panic population, chiefly Mexican, their culture palpably visible south of West Sixteenth Street between South Halsted Street and South Western Avenue. Yet the very name harks back to the Czech immigrants who settled the district shortly after the great fire. They were followed by Polish and Yugoslavian immigrants. The Czechs later moved south and west, often to Berwyn and Cicero. Here and there in Pilsen, ancient legends and signs engraved on the upper stories of buildings bear out their eastern European origins, and comparable testimony is evident in the facades of the many apartment buildings and storefronts that are surmounted by the step gables common to much of the architecture of the Bohemian towns of Europe.

The extent of the change in the composition of the district, most of that dating from the post–World War II years, may be observed by driving or walking along West Eighteenth Street, one of Chicago's liveliest and most colorful thoroughfares. Ironically, the owners of shops, bars, and other commercial establishments in the area have never been wealthy enough to tear down their old buildings and replace them with new ones, with the happy result that the street conveys much of the architectural flavor of decades past. The Mexican Fine Arts Center Museum at 1852 West Nineteenth Street, occupying a space in Harrison Park, was built as a natatorium in 1913, after designs by William Carbys Zimmerman. Converted into a commercial building in the 1930s, and enlarged in the late 1980s and early 1990s, the museum functions today as a neighborhood center where exhibitions and comparable cultural events are central to the life of the community. Among the most striking buildings nearby is St. Adalbert Roman Catholic Church at 1650 West Seventeenth Street, designed by Henry J. Schlacks in 1914 in Renaissance Revival mode. Originally meant for Polish immigrants, it now serves a Hispanic congregation.

The Hispanic identity of Pilsen notwithstanding, it owes a further measure of its vitality to the colony of painters and sculptors who have established their homes and studios there during the course of the last generation.

2127 West Twenty-second Place

ARCHITECT: Henry J. Schlacks

One of the most prolific church architects in pre–World War II Chicago, Schlacks designed in a wide assortment of historical styles. One of his smaller but altogether rewarding efforts is St. Paul's. Commissioned by a German parish on the near southwest side, the twin-spired building is remarkable for its well-crafted use of brick, a material common to much German Gothic architecture. The interior is especially notable for its decorative features, including mosaics over the chancel arch and numerous statues of sacred figures and groups, chief among them a marble series depicting the fourteen stations of the cross.

[*119*] **On Leong Chinese Merchants Association** (1927)

2216 South Wentworth Avenue

ARCHITECTS: Michaelsen & Rognstad

The businessman's group for whom this building was constructed was formed early in the twentieth century. With the nearby gate providing symbolic entrance to Chicago's Chinatown, the On Leong is a prominent example of a theme building. A casual stroll before dim sum or after dinner will demonstrate that many of the buildings in the neighborhood also display references to Chinese architecture, art, and culture. The pagoda-topped corner pavilions of the On Leong are linked across the facade by shops, arcades, and porches along the three-story front. Chinatown itself has expanded north of Cermak Road in recent years as the rail yards formerly there have been transformed to commercial and residential use.

350 East Twenty-second Street

ARCHITECTS: Howard Van Doren Shaw (1912, 1917, 1924);
Charles Z. Klauder (1931)

The Donnelley Company returned to Howard Van Doren Shaw when they
needed to expand operations beyond their Lakeside Press Building (39).
Again Shaw used the history and imagery of printing as the basis for a
rich surface ornamentation. The new building, adjacent to the tracks of
the Illinois Central Railroad, received raw materials and distributed finished products at a vastly larger scale than before, marking the city's
great industrial growth. The large, heavy presses required long spans and
high ceilings. Resting on a limestone base, the projecting brick piers of
the main block of the building emphasize the mass of the building, although the large areas of glass allowed an abundant amount of natural
light for workers at the presses within. The offices of the company were
here as well, and a series of richly detailed public and administrative
spaces, including a spectacular vaulted upper-level library, were located
on the southern facade. While still headquartered in Chicago, most of the
company's printing has been moved to new plants. In 1999 plans were
announced to use the building as the Lakeside Technology Center for Internet services in the expanding markets of electronic commerce.

South Lake Shore Drive and Twenty-third Street

ARCHITECTS: C. F. Murphy & Associates (1971); Skidmore, Owings & Merrill (1986); Thompson, Ventulett, Stainback & Associates, with A. Epstein & Sons International (1996)

This immense complex of exposition halls has had a tempestuous history as well as a steadily changing appearance, the latter due mostly to the constant and growing need for commercial exhibition space in a city traditionally known as a national convention center. The opening of McCormick Place in 1960 was accompanied by a chorus of complaints, in the meantime never fully abated, about its siting on a lakefront Chicagoans have long sought to keep open and free. The original building, by Shaw, Metz & Associates, was an uninspired effort destroyed—mercifully, some would say—by fire in 1967. The later decision to put up a new building on the same site had at least the consoling effect of leading to the impressive, decidedly superior structure now known as McCormick Place East. Its massive trussed roof and recessed glass walls recall Mies van der Rohe's National Gallery in Berlin, an association traceable to the experience the chief designer, Gene Summers, had in Mies's office before he joined C. F. Murphy & Associates.

In 1986 the need for expanded space led to the construction of a second hall, by Skidmore, Owings & Merrill, across Lake Shore Drive to the west. Known as McCormick Place North, the building's roof is supported by cables attached to the two rows of six huge pylons. It also betrays a Miesian influence in the treatment of the surface of its four opaque metal facades, where triangulated lines expressive of the interior roof trusses recall Mies's unbuilt 1953 Convention Hall. Here the homage is less successful than in the 1971 building, mostly on account of indifferent proportioning and detailing, with the further unhappy result that McCormick Place East and North bear little visual kinship.

Even less similarity is apparent in the third structure, called McCormick Place South and completed in 1996 from the plans of Thompson, Ventulett, Stainback & Associates of Atlanta, with A. Epstein & Sons International of Chicago. It is an enormous affair, boasting a single hall of 840,000 square feet, which some publicists have called the largest room

in the world. Functionally the current McCormick Place is capable of achieving its principal end, namely, attracting more expositions to the city than can be claimed by any of Chicago's rivals, principally Atlanta, New York City, Las Vegas, and Orlando (until one of them builds a still larger hall). As architecture, McCormick Place suffers from a gigantism unalleviated by the scattered massing of the new addition. Worse still is the motley look now conveyed by the entire three-part ensemble.

In 1998 a thirty-three-story hotel was added by the same architects who were responsible for McCormick Place South. Both later buildings manifestly share a lack of distinction, despite an effort to vivify the shaft of the hotel by crowning it with a massively projecting roof and by superimposing an outcropping on the facade.

[*122*] **Prairie Avenue Historic District**

1800 and 1900 blocks of South Prairie Avenue, 1800 block of South Indiana Avenue, and 211–217 East Cullerton Street

Prairie Avenue, "the sunny street of the sifted few," is today an outdoor museum of urban change. The houses of George Pullman, Marshall Field, Philip Armour, among others, lined the street, making it one of the finest neighborhoods in the city. Yet its life, begun after the Civil War, was short. The tracks of the Illinois Central Railroad to the east of the district changed from a symbol of modern enterprise to a source of constant noise and pollution with the enormous growth in traffic. To its west the

railroads needed warehousing. This led to redevelopment of that area into a zone of rail yards, warehouses, and, later, an automobile row along Michigan Avenue. Though the neighborhood only had a life of two generations, it remains the symbolic home of the city's most important leaders between the Civil War and World War I. Eleven houses from this period survive.

While the houses of Pullman, Armour, and Field are gone, survivors include Solon S. Beman's W. W. Kimball House (1892), a splendid limestone example of the French château mode then popular. It is today the headquarters of the U.S. Soccer Foundation. Other surviving buildings include the Glessner (123), Coleman-Ames, and Keith Houses, as well as the relocated and restored Clarke House (124). The Glessner House Museum is the principal organization pursuing the interpretation of the district. The Eastman Kodak Company regional office and warehouse at the northeast corner of Eighteenth and Indiana, designed in 1906 by Hill &

Woltersdorf, indicates the speed and scale of the transformation of the neighborhood. At the southeast corner of that intersection is the former Swiss Products building, now adaptively reused as the Vietnam Veterans Art Museum. The open space between the Glessner and Clarke Houses had been named for Hillary Rodham Clinton in honor of her commitment to historic preservation. First lady to President Bill Clinton at the time of its renaming, she is a native of Park Ridge, a northwest suburb. It has since been renamed the Chicago Women's Park and Garden. In the surrounding area, as industrial and commercial uses have waned, many existing buildings have been converted to residential use and an increasing number of dwellings have been constructed.

[*123*] **Glessner House** (1887)
1800 South Prairie Avenue
ARCHITECT: Henry Hobson Richardson

Two of Richardson's finest designs were realized in Chicago: the Marshall Field Wholesale Store and the John and Frances Glessner House, both finished in 1887. The former was razed in 1930; the latter was saved from demolition in 1966 only by the concerted efforts of a group of private citizens led by several architects, including Harry Weese and Ben Weese of Chicago and Philip Johnson of New York. Thus the Glessner House has been not only a standing architectural treasure but also an arena for the ongoing preservation debate of the last few decades. Today this is the only Richardson design open to the public that shows his concept of the complete integration of exterior and interior design.

Richardson's creative habits often favored the use of heavy rusticated masonry reminiscent of the Romanesque period. He employed this approach consciously and emphatically in the Glessner House, since his clients desired a residence that conveyed an image of enduring strength. And so it does, with its expanse of powerful walls of layered ashlar, its massive arches, and its overall spareness of ornament.

In the interior, however, a contrasting warmth and intimacy appropriate to the privacy of the inhabitants are perceptible in generously scaled spaces dressed in rich woods, patterned wallpapers and textiles, veined

marbles, and decorative tiles. Richardson was not content to entrust the interior to assistants, so he supervised it himself. Each principal room contains a major piece or group of furniture designed by, or through, him. He also convinced the Glessners of the value of William Morris's Arts and Crafts movement. The influence can be seen in the decorative program of the house.

Following its rescue in 1966, the house became the property of the Chicago School of Architecture Foundation, later the Chicago Architecture Foundation, then the Prairie Avenue House Museums, and now the Glessner House Museum, all of which have pursued a program of preservation and restoration. Beginning in 1984, a careful program of cleaning and tuckpointing the exterior masonry began with the exterior granite, revealing its pink cast and glittering flecks of mica and feldspar. By 2000 the roof tiles, interior brick walls and limestone sills, lintels, and stairs were cleaned. Windows and their frames have been repaired or restored, and the courtyard has been regraded to its original contour. All the principal rooms, and many of the subsidiary spaces, have been restored or interpreted to their original state, although one space on the second floor, which had included Mrs. Glessner's conservatory, became a conference room in 1976. Hammond, Beeby & Babka did this work in a contemporary manner.

1855 South Indiana Avenue
ARCHITECT: unknown

The oldest building in Chicago is now on its third site. Henry and Caroline Clarke, immigrants from upstate New York, built their timber-framed Greek Revival pavilion near present-day Michigan Avenue and Sixteenth Street, on a property extending eastward to the lakeshore. The Doric-columned porch, center entrance plan, triple sash windows, broad cornice boards, and high ceilings were typical elements of Greek Revival dwellings familiar to the Clarkes before they moved to Chicago. The Italianate cupola was added in the 1850s. Shortly after the great fire in 1871, the house was moved south to Indiana Avenue and Forty-fifth Street, where it served for many years as the parish house for the St. Paul Church of God in Christ, an African American congregation. In 1977 it was moved to its present site as part of the development of the Prairie

Avenue Historic District. That move included a thrilling moment when the house was lifted up and over the elevated tracks of the city's rapid transit system. Following this move, the house, both exterior and interior, has been painstakingly restored to the first years of its existence, although the window glass is incorrect. A gallery interpreting the early settlement of Chicago and the intervening years of the house's history is included in its newly constructed basement. The landscaping near the house has been replanted based on typical use of the time as well as surviving documentary evidence.

[*125*] **Second Presbyterian Church** (1874)
1936 South Michigan Avenue
ARCHITECTS: James Renwick; remodeled, Howard Van Doren Shaw (1901)

If Prairie Avenue was the sunny street of the sifted few, this is where the light, carefully modulated by elegant art-glass windows, found them of a Sunday morning. Appropriate to the congregation's ambition, a New York architect—remembered for his Smithsonian Institution in the Mall in

Washington and St. Patrick's Cathedral on Fifth Avenue in New York—designed their 1851 building in the Loop and, after it was destroyed in the great 1871 fire, the present building in 1874. Renwick used the Gothic Revival because of its associations with British ecclesiastical forms, and a local limestone marked with bits of bitumen, which led to each church being nicknamed the Spotted Church.

Following a 1900 fire, Chicagoan Howard Van Doren Shaw repaired the building, designed a new roof with a clerestory over the nave, and oversaw the mural cycle by Frederick Clay Bartlett. He also supervised the installation (or reinstallation) of art-glass windows from this and other sites by such admired designers as Edward Burne-Jones (whose two windows had been fabricated by fellow Englishman William Morris) and Americans from the Tiffany company in New York, McCully & Miles, and Louis Millet.

[*126*] **Bronzeville**

Quinn Chapel (1892)
2401 South Wabash Avenue
ARCHITECT: Henry F. Starbuck

Chicago Defender Building (1936)
2400 South Michigan Avenue
ARCHITECT: Philip B. Maher

Pilgrim Baptist Church (1891)
3301 South Indiana Avenue
ARCHITECTS: Adler & Sullivan

Eighth Regiment Armory (1915)
3533 South Giles Avenue
ARCHITECT: J. B. Dibelka

Operation PUSH (1921)
930 East Fiftieth Street
ARCHITECT: Alfred S. Alschuler

The principal architectural monuments of the expanding African American community in Chicago illustrate the segregated growth pattern of the community and the role that succession plays in actual reuse of

buildings. The *Chicago Defender* currently occupies a building first constructed for the Illinois Automobile Club. Earlier, it occupied another building (3435 South Indiana Avenue) converted from its original use. The Eighth Regiment Armory, the first such building erected for African American servicemen in a segregated army, has been recently rehabilitated and converted for use as the Bronzeville Military Academy by the Chicago Public Schools. Quinn Chapel has been the sanctuary of Chicago's oldest African Methodist Episcopal congregation since its construction. Founded in 1844 and formally organized in 1847, the congregation has played an important role in the life of the city since its efforts for abolition. The buildings currently occupied by Pilgrim Baptist Church and Operation PUSH were first constructed for the principally German Jewish KAM congregation. (Kehilath Anshe Ma'ariv means in Hebrew "the congregation of men in the west.") As the congregation, the oldest in Chicago, grew, its members continued to move from the center to the periphery, in this case along a southerly radius. KAM/Pilgrim Baptist includes three brilliant elements typical of the Adler & Sullivan partnership—exquisite acoustics, elegant ornamentation, and efficient planning. Pilgrim Baptist is also distinguished for having had Dr. Thomas Dorsey as musical director. Dorsey is recognized as the creator of gospel music, and the choir he developed at Pilgrim Baptist included Mahalia Jackson among its members. Operation PUSH, one of the most visible and successful of the institutions created in the wake of the civil rights movement, acquired the Second KAM when that congregation merged with Congregation Isaiah Israel and moved to its current site, also designed by Alschuler, in 1971.

[*127*] Illinois Institute of Technology (1939–)

South State Street, between Thirty-first and Thirty-fifth Streets,
bounded on the west by Federal Street and on the east by
Michigan Avenue

ARCHITECTS: Ludwig Mies van der Rohe; associated architects
at different times: Holabird & Root; Friedman, Alschuler & Sincere;
PACE Associates; Murphy/Jahn; Skidmore, Owings & Merrill; Lohan
Associates; Rem Koolhaas

Mies had a very long time to design this campus: he began the project in
1939, and he finished the first main campus building in 1946 (after two
research buildings constructed during World War II). In this period Mies
shifted from a design process concerned with expression of function to
one centered on the expression of structure. His American manner
emerged only after long and profound reflection and formed the basis of
his designs for the remainder of his career.

His buildings on the campus demonstrate four variations on the
structural theme. The regular steel frame, tightly bound, enclosed with
taut panels of brick and glass, predominates, as in Alumni, Perlstein,
Wishnick, and Siegel Halls. The concrete frame of the three apartment
towers sees these same ideas expressed in a high-rise. The bearing-wall

brick of the chapel encloses a focused, symmetrical, directional space unique on the campus. The chapel has recently been rehabilitated. The unitary space created by the exoskeletal structure of S. R. Crown Hall is one of Mies's most beautiful expressions of the pavilion temple. The Commons is an earlier study of the same idea.

The campus plan itself is an arrangement of form and space where the buildings and the spaces between them engage in a stately dialogue in which solid and void, plane and enclosure, interact to create a serene harmony of components. Mies's elegant progressions of symmetry and asymmetry—where a symmetrical whole will divide into asymmetrical halves, which are themselves composed of symmetrical units, likewise composed of asymmetrical elements—provide a variety of experience unexpected in forms that seem at first so severe.

Mies was dismissed as campus architect in 1958. Afterward, Skidmore, Owings & Merrill added several buildings, among them the library and student union, sited according to Mies's plan but otherwise unsuccessful. A later building of distinction is Keating Hall (1966), designed by Myron Goldsmith of Skidmore, Owings & Merrill.

In 1998 the Institute decided to renew the campus by securing a new master plan from Lohan Associates, sponsoring a design competition for a new student center and developing a new landscape plan for the campus. The McCormick Tribune Campus Center competition commission was given to Rem Koolhaas of OMA in the Netherlands and is scheduled for completion in 2003. Located along the east side of State Street between Thirty-second and Thirty-third Streets, the new building is marked by a stainless steel tube enclosing the elevated tracks and much use of a bright orange. Koolhaas won the Pritzker Architecture Prize for 2000. Michael Van Valkenburgh Associates prepared the landscape plan, in association with Peter Lindsay Schaudt Landscape Architecture, and was influenced by the example of landscape planting developed for the campus by Alfred Caldwell in cooperation with Mies. Schaudt began to implement the plan in 1999, with work to extend over several years. To the south of the student center, between Thirty-third and Thirty-fourth Streets, Helmut Jahn's firm Murphy/Jahn has won a limited competition in late 2001 to erect new student housing. With curving roofs and shiny curtain walls, the series of six elements will be first occupied in fall 2003.

The Institute has also developed market-rate housing east of the campus. Optima, the firm of IIT architecture professor David Hovey, won the commission and occupancy began in late 2001.

[*128*] **St. Gabriel Church** (1888)
4501 South Lowe Avenue
ARCHITECTS: Burnham & Root

St. Gabriel's is an Irish Catholic immigrant church near the former stockyards. Its founding, savvy, and beloved priest, Maurice Dorney, secured support for his building campaign from members of the stockyards' leadership. The son-in-law of one of these leaders was Daniel Burnham, whose partner, John Wellborn Root, designed this taut exercise in the brick Romanesque popular at the time, especially through the example of H. H. Richardson. Few immigrant neighborhood churches were so fortunate in securing the services of a high-style architect for their needs. The turreted tower attached to its right balances the broad triangle of Root's facade. Although the entry has been extended forward and the tower shortened since the church was first built, it retains the clarity and

simplicity of its initial construction. In her biography of her brother-in-law, the poet Harriet Monroe said that Root's manner here was "as personal as the clasp of his hand."

[*129*] **Kenwood District**
Between East Forty-seventh and East Fifty-first Streets, South Blackstone Avenue and South Drexel Boulevard

There is nothing better than a tour of Kenwood to provide the visitor with a sense of the residential polish that marked parts of Chicago's South Side during the decades between the great fire and the depression. This district, which was a suburb from its founding in the 1850s until its annexation by the city in 1889, was home to families wealthy enough to build a substantial number of ample, tastefully composed houses, many of which are still in evidence today. Various styles represent the talents of some of the best architects active at the time in Chicago. Notable among

the surviving buildings whose designers are known are the Tudor Revival house at 4815 South Woodlawn (1910), by Howard Van Doren Shaw; the Georgian Revival house at 4858 South Dorchester (1897), by Handy & Cady; and the Renaissance Revival house at 4900 South Ellis (1899), by Horatio Wilson and Benjamin Marshall.

Some of the handsomest residences are by now-anonymous builders, too many to be cited here. At the same time, one of the designers is nothing if not famous: Frank Lloyd Wright, represented by two early houses standing side by side, both dating from 1892. The Warren McArthur House at 4852 South Kenwood is an eclectic mixture, while the neo-Georgian exterior of the George Blossom House at 4858 South Kenwood gives no hint of the strikingly original spaces inside. The Blossom coach house, dating from 1907, is far closer to Wright's mature style.

It is worth recalling that both houses were designed while Wright was employed by Louis Sullivan and Dankmar Adler, who presumed that he would devote his energies exclusively to their commissions. When it was discovered that Wright had been moonlighting on Kenwood Avenue and elsewhere, he was dismissed from the firm. Even so, his influence soon grew great enough to be felt in the design of several houses in Kenwood. The most noteworthy of these is the Magerstadt House (1908), at 4930

South Greenwood, by George W. Maher. The Julius Rosenwald House (1903), at 4901 South Ellis, by Nimmons and Fellows, also bears a debt to the Prairie style.

[**130**] **Atrium Houses** (1961)
1370 East Madison Park
ARCHITECT: Y. C. Wong

Among the most ancient of building types are dwellings that are closed to the street and have an atrium open to the sky at their centers. Y. C. Wong organized eight such units on Madison Park, a quiet residential mews rare in Chicago, creating in each a serene environment. Wong was a student of Ludwig Mies van der Rohe at the Illinois Institute of Technology and learned there how many possibilities this venerable house form still possessed. Mies had made many studies of courtyard houses beginning in the 1930s. A uniform roof plate caps the simply expressed brick panel walls of the exterior, uniting the two sets of four dwellings. The passage dividing these two halves repeats on a modest pedestrian scale the boulevard that defines the public character of Madison Park. The interi-

ors of each unit share the atrium as the principal source of daylight and the opportunity to enjoy the visually continuous but environmentally distinct spaces. This experience is perhaps most satisfying on a sunny winter's day. A low raking sun fills the interiors with warmth, revealing a beautiful contrast between the snow resting on the various elements of the courtyard, which in turn obscure and reveal their inner character.

[*131*] **Heller House** (1897)

5132 South Woodlawn Avenue
ARCHITECT: Frank Lloyd Wright

As with his other work from the 1890s, Wright explores many ideas and possibilities in this design. The narrow side of the house is pushed well back from the street, and one enters midway along the long side on the south. The entry leads into a stair hall with principal spaces to left and right, and a planar stair above, similar to the parti he had used with Sullivan at the Charnley House (90). In the living and dining rooms, walls step out and ceilings step up, providing ideas of expansion unexpected from the strongly bounded planes encountered on the exterior. The walls are built up of the preferred urban materials of the time—limestone base,

tan Roman brick walls, and tawny molded plaster high-relief panels of female figures (designed by sculptor Richard Bock) under the hovering
roof.

[*132*] **St. Thomas the Apostle** (1924)
5472 South Kimbark Avenue
ARCHITECT: Barry Byrne

The modernist manner of Byrne's design is worth noting in view of the
fact that this church was built at a time when most American ecclesiastical architecture was faithfully based on traditional forms. The concealed
steel beams that hold up the roof make possible the remarkable ampli-

tude of the 95-by-193-foot worship space, while the openness of that effect is underscored by the sleek, abstracted patterns of the ceiling design and the boldly original contours of the alcoves. A substantial quantity of terra-cotta ornament is mounted along the cornice and around exterior surfaces of windows and doorways, although it is of an exotic rather than conventional order. The most arresting components of the interior decorative program are the bronze bas-reliefs of the stations of the cross, interpreted in the Art Deco mode by the Italian-born American sculptor Alfeo Faggi.

[*133*] **Keck-Gottschalk-Keck Apartments** (1937)
5551 South University Avenue
A R C H I T E C T S : George F. and William Keck

This modestly scaled apartment building is one of the earliest examples in Chicago of the modern architecture associated with the International

Style. As such it relies for its effect on a clarity of composition and an abstracted rectilinear form, both precluding the ornament still commonly practiced at the time by designers in the Art Deco mode.

[*134*] **Promontory Apartments** (1949)

5530 South Shore Drive
ARCHITECTS: Ludwig Mies van der Rohe; PACE Associates;
Holsman, Holsman & Klekamp

Mies's first tall building launched his important relationship with developer Herbert Greenwald. Its twenty-one-story exposed-concrete frame can be seen stepping back at the sixth, eleventh, and sixteenth floors, demonstrating the reduced load to be carried as the building rose. The glass-enclosed entrance lobby and portes cochere at either end of the facade contribute to the illusion of the building being lifted off the ground, allowing the horizontal flow of space at the ground plane. The broad main

slab of the building is only two bays deep, emphasizing that the single view of the residents is toward the lake. As he had done in his first American buildings on the IIT campus, Mies used an exposed frame and filled the simple enclosed panels with brick below and glass above. The simplicity and clarity of form and the rigorously limited palette of materials demonstrate that the principal effect of the building derives from the subtle play of light and shade against the plane of the whole facade.

[*135*] **Museum of Science and Industry** (1893)

South Lake Shore Drive at East Fifty-seventh Street
ARCHITECTS: D. H. Burnham & Co.; reconstruction, Graham, Anderson, Probst & White (1929–40)

Students of Chicago and its architecture may find the history of the Museum of Science and Industry as instructive as the extraordinary collection of objects, devices, and displays suggested by the institution's name. The museum is the sole major surviving remnant of the city's celebrated World's Columbian Exposition of 1893, where it functioned as the Palace of Fine Arts. After the fair closed, it took on a new role as the home of the Field Museum of Natural History, serving in that capacity until the latter moved in 1920 to new quarters in Grant Park (13).

The original edifice, designed principally by Burnham & Company's Charles Atwood, was the Columbian Exposition's only fire-protected structure, but like its counterparts, it had been constructed of a substance called staff, a plaster compound reinforced by fiber, cheap to make but markedly impermanent. By the end of the 1920s, the whole building was in a state of acute deterioration.

It then found a vital new function, chiefly as a consequence of the generosity and vision of a Chicago businessman, Julius Rosenwald. On a previous visit to Munich, Rosenwald had been entranced by that city's splendid Deutsches Museum, a surpassingly varied collection of scientific and technological displays that inspired him to promote the creation of a similar museum in Chicago. With the help of other Chicagoans as well as the city's government, Rosenwald contributed more than $7 million toward the transformation of the Atwood building into a new one, mostly by the replacement of the original exterior substance with an appropriately long-lasting material, Bedford limestone. An administrative staff was assembled, collections and displays were gathered, and the museum was opened in 1933.

As is evident today, Atwood's design was true to the Beaux-Arts classicist aesthetic that dominated the Columbian Exposition. As such, it was

freely indebted to the uses of the ancient past, most apparently in the elevations, where the caryatid columns of the porches and the reliefs of lapiths and centaurs, taken respectively from Athens's Erechtheion and Parthenon, were added to an overall reliance on the Ionic order. The dome, harking back to Roman precedent, occupies the center of the structure, thus signaling Atwood's reemployment of that major attribute of the Beaux-Arts rationale, a rigorously axial plan.

The reconstruction of the exterior was carried out, in several phases between 1929 and 1940, by Graham, Anderson, Probst & White. The interior, also reconstituted progressively, in the late 1930s, by Shaw, Naess & Murphy, is notable for its Art Deco manner, popular at that time. In 1986 a domed structure enclosing the 342-seat Omnimax Theater was built along the museum's east elevation. The architects were Hammell, Green & Abrahamson of Minneapolis.

[*136*] **Robie House** (1910)
5757 South Woodlawn Avenue
ARCHITECT: Frank Lloyd Wright

The Robie House is among the most famous in the world. Wright's 1908 design for Frederick C. Robie, a bicycle manufacturer and early automobile aficionado, was completed by associates of the architect after Wright abandoned his practice and family in September 1909. Robie and

his family took up residence in the house in 1910. The interpenetration of masses, volumes, and spaces; the insistent horizontal extension of the forms and overhanging, often cantilevered, roofs; the abstract conventionalization of natural forms in the ranks of art-glass windows; the furniture that repeated the forms of the building, and in groups defined their own spaces; the colors linked to an autumnal prairie palette—all combine, along with some brilliant photographs and drawings of the building, to establish the Robie House as seminal in both Wright's work and modern architecture.

The Robies lived in the house for only a short time, and it came into the hands of the Chicago Theological Seminary by the 1930s. Since then, it has rarely been used for residential purposes. Recently the University of Chicago, now its owner, the National Trust for Historic Preservation, and the Frank Lloyd Wright Preservation Trust (until then focused on Wright's Oak Park Home and Studio) agreed to restore the house and operate it as a historic house museum. The careful restoration is projected to be complete by 2007, permitting visitors a rare glimpse inside some of the exacting process. When complete, the Robie House dining-room furniture, designed by Wright, should be returned from the university's Smart Museum of Art, where it may be seen until then.

The strikingly horizontal exterior image illustrating this entry is the result of a precise collaboration between Aaron Siskind and Richard Nickel, whereby they placed their cameras so that the two negatives matched perfectly edge to edge, and could then produce a single, exact image.

[*137*] **University of Chicago** (1891–)
Bounded by Fifty-fifth and Sixty-first Streets, the Illinois Central tracks and Cottage Grove Avenue

The major phases of the university's architectural history can be readily discerned from a walk around the campus. The two most obvious are the earliest and the latest, separated by slightly more than a century. In 1891 a plan of the newly founded school was conceived by two of its trustees, Martin Ryerson and Charles L. Hutchinson, and plotted by Chicago architect Henry Ives Cobb. An area bounded by Fifty-seventh Street, University Avenue, Fifty-ninth Street, and Ellis Avenue was divided into seven quadrangles. That space, now known as the Main Quadrangles and clearly perceptible as the heart of the university, was outfitted with buildings based on the English Gothic model of Oxford University. Several of the early components of the grouping were designed by Cobb himself, the oldest of them Cobb Hall (1891, named for a benefactor, not the architect), and Ryerson Physical Laboratory and Kent Chemical Laboratory, each dating from 1894. Following the turn of the twentieth century, Shepley, Rutan & Coolidge were appointed campus architects. That firm had earlier employed the classical idiom in its designs for the Chicago Public Library (now the Chicago Cultural Center [9]) and the Art Institute of Chicago (12), but at the university, its architects remained true to Cobb's Gothic style, notably in William Rainey Harper Memorial Library (1912), the Hutchinson Court and Tower Group (1903), and Bartlett Gymnasium (1903). Thereafter, commissions were awarded to various offices for individual buildings, but the Gothic manner was kept intact. Holabird & Roche was responsible for Rosenwald Hall (1915), and Coolidge & Hodgson (successor firm to Shepley, Rutan & Coolidge) for the intimate, richly decorated Bond Chapel (1926).

The most monumental edifice on the campus is Rockefeller Memorial Chapel (1928), designed by one of the major masters of the American Gothic Revival of the 1920s, Bertram G. Goodhue, and named for John D. Rockefeller, the industrialist whose enormous wealth was sufficient to guarantee the founding of the university. Just north and west of the chapel is a museum of Near Eastern antiquities, the Oriental Institute (1931), by Mayes, Murray & Phillips, successors to the Goodhue office.

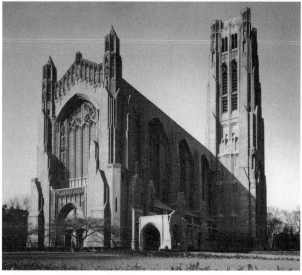

The interruption of building activity by the depression and World War II had a major effect on American architecture as a whole and no less on later additions to the university. The traditional reliance on the Gothic gave way to modernist styles, with the result that recent campus buildings bear the mark more of their individual designers than of any shared stylistic approach. That development has led to some impressive work, but at the expense of the commonality of vision that made the pre-1930 Main Quadrangles and contiguous areas a campus equal in quality to the finest in America.

The last recognizable effort in the Gothic is the Administration Building (Holabird, Root & Burgee, 1948), a structure with little to recommend it beyond a tolerable compatibility with its neighbors. In 1955 Eero Saarinen was asked to produce another master plan, the first since 1891. Addressed principally to the land south of Sixtieth Street, its chief adornments there were Mies van der Rohe's Social Service Administration Building (1965) and Saarinen's own Law School complex (1960), the latter including a low-rise classroom wing, an auditorium building in the shape of an eight-pointed star, and the Law School library, identifiable by its folded glass wall. Edward Durell Stone's Graduate Residence Hall, its columns unimpressively thin, is one of the least successful of the Sixtieth Street group. Saarinen's master plan also resulted in the construction of an ensemble of buildings on the North Campus, all related to the arts: the Cochrane-Woods Arts Center, including the Smart Museum of Art (Edward Larrabee Barnes, 1974), and the Court Theatre (Harry Weese, 1981).

At the end of the 1990s, the university undertook a full-scale examination of its values and priorities and the architecture reflective of them, with the effort leading to a third master plan. This one, assembled by a committee of university personnel and guided by planners Naramore, Bain, Brady & Johansen, is meant to be as comprehensive as any comparable endeavor previous to it. Nearly a dozen major new buildings or reconstituted old ones are anticipated. They will be located in accordance with a reorganization of the campus framework that promises all passages to be appropriately landscaped. The first phase of the new master plan will expand and integrate the northern portion of the campus. Among the chief components there are two structures designed by Cesar Pelli & Associates: a large parking structure (finished in 2001) and the Gerald Ratner Athletics Center (completion anticipated in 2003), the latter meant to replace the attractive but antiquated Bartlett Gymnasium, which in turn will be transformed into a student center, equipped with a dining facility. Neighboring buildings are the Interdivisional Research

Building for the Physical Sciences and Biological Sciences Divisions, by Ellenzweig Associates (completion targeted for 2005), and the Max Palevsky Residential Commons, by Ricardo Legorreta (finished in 2001). The Ellenzweig and Legorreta buildings are part of a consolidation into quadrangle form of two areas already in existence. In the first instance, the residence halls will be sited just north of Regenstein Library (1970, Skidmore, Owings & Merrill, lead designer Walter Netsch), a structure whose grooved and roughened limestone walls are indebted to the primarily British Brutalist movement of the 1960s and 1970s. The Interdivisional Research Building will complete a quadrangle whose members are associated with the natural sciences: the Kersten Physics Teaching Center (1985, Holabird & Root and Harold H. Hellman, university architect); the John Crerar Library (1984, Stubbins Associates), a respectable modernist effort; and two idiosyncratic works by I. W. Colburn: the Henry Hinds Laboratory for the Geophysical Sciences (1968), in collaboration with J. Lee Jones, and the Cummings Life Science Center (1973), in collaboration with Schmidt, Garden & Erikson and Harold H. Hellman.

One of the major new buildings, the Graduate School of Business, designed by Raphael Viñoly, will replace Eero Saarinen's Woodward Court and Commons student housing complex east of the Main Quadrangles (anticipated completion 2004). Under consideration for a still later date is an arts center that, added to the Court Theatre and the Cochrane-Woods Arts Center, would complete an arts quadrangle on the North Campus.

Among the newly completed buildings, the idiom is mostly modernist, with the Palevsky Commons notable for its colorful exterior. The palette is bright and emphatically cheerful, but its proximity to Henry Moore's 1967 sculpture, *Nuclear Energy*, palpably suggestive of an atomic explosion, makes for a jarring contextual contrast.

Meanwhile, several of the new additions preserve a more traditional outer appearance. The University of Chicago Press Building, for one, is a conservative masonry building finished in 2000 by Booth Hansen Associates at Sixtieth Street and Dorchester Avenue, on the southeast edge of the campus. The massing, the ashlar limestone envelope, and the vertical fenestration of the Kovler Gymnasium of the university's Laboratory School (2000), by Nagle Hartray Danker Kagan McKay, are reminders of the Gothicism of the old campus.

From its placement on Fifty-ninth Street, the Lab School looks out upon one of the most splendid spaces on the campus, the Midway Plaisance, a quarter-mile-wide parkland, planned as early as the 1870s by Frederick Law Olmsted but remembered more as the area of the 1893 World's Columbian Exposition devoted to the pavilions of foreign nations. The Midway is now owned by the city of Chicago and managed by the Chicago Park District, but both entities have cooperated in the university's decisions to make the space more active and socially inviting. The year-round ice-skating rink and its warming house, completed in 2001 by Nagle Hartray Danker Kagan McKay, make up the principal parts of that program, which in final form will feature a number of elegantly plotted gardens. Moreover, in keeping with the recomposition of the Midway, additional landscaping as well as architectural decorative elements lined along Ellis Avenue are intended to turn that thoroughfare into the visual spine of the campus.

South Shore Cultural Center (1906, 1916)
(Originally South Shore Country Club)
7059 South Shore Drive
ARCHITECTS: Marshall & Fox

Nothing is more impressive about the South Shore Cultural Center than the splendid grounds it occupies on the lakefront. They are reminders of the opulence of the private facility opened in 1906 as the South Shore Country Club. In those days this area was far enough from downtown to qualify as "country," and its membership included some of the city's wealthiest and most distinguished citizens. The growth of the club called not only for the clubhouse, but for a later, substantially larger addition, also by Marshall & Fox, and completed in 1916. Following the 1960s shift in the demographics of the neighborhood, the club closed. The Chicago Park District acquired the building, intending initially to demolish it, but a group calling itself the Coalition to Save the South Shore Country Club advanced the idea of turning it into a cultural center that would serve the entire public. In 1978 the Park District decided in the coalition's favor, and funds were secured to renovate the building and establish the South Shore Cultural Center.

Today access is gained through an attractive forecourt flanked by pergolas. By contrast with the main structure's plain stucco facades, the colorful, classically ornamented interior comes as a lively and rewarding surprise. It consists of a spacious corridor that runs from a large ballroom reception area on the north, past a solarium on the east, to a theater on

the south that is named after the late and multitalented actor-singer-athlete Paul Robeson.

Restoration of the complex continues, with much of the exterior and interior work having been done by an office of the Chicago Park District, and most of the interior by Norman DeHaan.

[*139*] **South Pullman District** (1880–94)
South Cottage Grove Avenue to South Langley Street between East 111th and East 115th Streets
ARCHITECTS: Solon S. Beman; Nathan F. Barrett

George Pullman invented the most successful railway sleeping car, and he wanted to conduct his vertically integrated manufacture in a site distant and secure from the corrupting influences of big cities. His comprehensively designed company town of Pullman, in then far southern Hyde Park (annexation to Chicago occurred in 1889), succeeded for about a decade, and then imploded in the depression, strike, and federal action that began in 1893.

The site consisted of roughly four hundred acres of land along the western shore of Lake Calumet close by the Illinois Central Railroad tracks. All the buildings were designed by Beman, and Barrett, a landscape architect, laid out the public spaces. Much of the original complex

has been demolished or damaged, including the 195-foot water tower that once dominated the town, the factory administration building and clock tower, and the Arcade with its remarkable interior spaces including stores, a bank, post office, library, and theater. Even so, the shape and substance of the community are still perceptible. The Hotel Florence—named for Pullman's daughter—has been restored and serves to welcome visitors to the community. Across the public square is the Green-stone Church, a crisp little variation on the Romanesque. The side streets are lined with row residences, originally more than fourteen hundred of them, mostly single-family units. A remarkable number, ranging from humble to elegant, have been preserved.

Wrigley Field (1914)

Clark and Addison Streets

ARCHITECT: Zachary Taylor Davis

Soldier Field (1925, 2003)

425 East McFetridge Drive, Lake Shore Drive below
Fourteenth Street

ARCHITECTS: Holabird & Roche; addition, Lohan Associates,
Wood & Zapata (2003)

U.S. Cellular Field (1991)

(Originally Comiskey Park)

Thirty-fifth Street and Shields Avenue

ARCHITECTS: Hellmuth, Obata & Kassabaum
Sports Facilities Group

United Center (1994)

1901 West Madison Street

ARCHITECTS: Hellmuth, Obata & Kassabaum
Sports Facilities Group

If Chicago's reputation for loyalties to its professional sports franchises is
exceptional among American cities, so was the age of the facilities in
which the reputation has been forged. Until old Comiskey Park was demolished and replaced by its namesake in 1991, and the Chicago Stadium replaced by the United Center in 1994, the 1929 Chicago Stadium
was the newest of the city's four major arenas.

Chicagoan Zachary Taylor Davis is best remembered for his designs
for the now-lost Comiskey Park and Wrigley Field. Those two steel-
framed, brick-enclosed structures are legendary for their fitness as ball-
parks in which the spectators were optimally close to the action. Wrigley
Field still exists, its nickname—"the friendly confines"—deriving largely
from its ivy-covered walls and ancient, hand-operated, but uncommonly
informative scoreboard.

Soldier Field, so-called in memory of Americans killed in World War I,
was designed for a capacity of 55,000, but it has been adapted to accommodate larger crowds, such as the more than 100,000 who viewed
the celebrated Jack Dempsey–Gene Tunney heavyweight championship

prize fight of 1927. Reflecting the neoclassical architecture of its neighbors, the Field Museum and the Shedd Aquarium, it is notable for the Doric columns that rise from the tops of the two long sides of its grandstands.

More recently, stadium owners seem driven by the desire for and economic benefit from transforming the communal nature of attending a sporting event into one where privilege and privacy are flaunted, and sports fans who also care about the built environment fear for the future. The competition for leisure dollars has led some owners of sports franchises in Chicago to destroy their historic homes and build new facilities. Both Comiskey Park (White Sox) and the Chicago Stadium (Blackhawks and Bulls) have been replaced by new facilities, on sites adjacent to their predecessors. In both cases, the conclusion of the new denizens of these facilities is that while it is easier to get and recycle a beer, in other ways the new facilities are exactly the soulless corporate hulks that were feared. Plans to make Comiskey more fan-friendly are now to be derived from the price of the naming rights for the now U.S. Cellular Field. Days after that announcement, U.S. Cellular, Inc., reported quarterly losses, giving rise to hopes or fears among fans that the new name would follow the path of Enron Field in Houston. At Soldier Field, a new seating bowl is being inserted within the colonnades in time for the 2003 season. Informed observers of the design and construction process are divided on whether the results will enhance or further damage the city's reputation for the quality of its sports facilities.

The Suburbs

The very word "suburb" implies a binary relationship: a small town satel-lite to a significantly larger one. Since World War II, the suburbs have fig-ured especially heavily in Chicago's history. The relationship of the city to its adjacent municipalities has undergone an unprecedented demo-graphic change. The population of the metropolitan area has steadily grown, and while that of the city has recently shown a slight increase, the suburbs continue to maintain their magnetism. For most of the last half-century, multitudes have elected to flee from the city's famous de-fects—poor schools, crowding, and unsafe streets high among them—hoping to find a greener physical setting and a sense of community that they believe the metropolis in all its presumed anonymity cannot pro-vide. There is evidence in the past decade of a reversal of this process, with Chicago exerting its own increased urbanistic magnetism (see pp. 171–72), but the powerful suburban drive has not been conclusively ar-rested.

Its goals, meanwhile, could not have been pursued without a means, which during the same period has taken on a form attractive enough to accelerate the process tremendously: the automobile. Affordable to buy and maintain by citizens of nearly all classes, and accommodated by a corresponding increase in the number of roads and highways, the car has proven integral to the American yearning for personal freedom, private ownership, material possession, and untrammeled mobility. To be sure, the average suburban motorist stuck in rush-hour traffic—which has also increased enormously in volume during the past several decades—may think of these assets less cordially. But in sum over the years, he or she has valued more than turned away from them, and this judgment, spurred by the car that finally brings its passengers home, has led to the rapid population growth of the postwar suburbs.

History offers the reminder, however, that exurban expansion and its effect on the built environment are hardly as recent as the post–World War II explosion. Chicago has spread outward from its ancient downtown in proportion to the evolution of transportation facilities. By the 1850s, less than two decades after the formal incorporation of Chicago, a single horse-drawn omnibus rolling on planked streets could carry a dozen or more people as far north as Lincoln Park. A few years later, similar but powered vehicles, moving twice as fast as a man could walk, operated on rails. Cable cars followed, and electric trains. By the time of the Chicago fire, railroads not only connected the central business district with such independent towns as Evanston, Hinsdale, Washington Heights, and Hyde Park, but enabled the inhabitants of those erstwhile far-flung places to work in the city. The railroad was the great instrument of suburban growth in Chicago and other older American cities long before the auto counted for anything. Rails radiated outward from downtown, and along the lines they traced, communities took form. Chicago was able to incorporate many of these (Hyde Park and Washington Heights among them), but after 1893 the city limits changed only a little, while existing suburbs grew and new ones were created.

Furthermore, the burgeoning of the city's outer metropolitan area between 1870 and 1940 was already significant enough to produce an architecture as important as it was various. Probably the most celebrated example is the body of revolutionary residential work of Frank Lloyd

Wright and his followers, the so-called Prairie school, that left its legacy most prominently in Oak Park, River Forest, and Riverside. But the more conservative house designs of David Adler and Howard Van Doren Shaw, principally in Lake Forest, and Benjamin Marshall in Libertyville merit attention in their own right.

Other architectural classifications are similarly worthy of note. Achievements in urban planning by Almerin Hotchkiss in laying out the plat of Lake Forest, by Frederick Law Olmsted in doing the same for Riverside, and by Solon S. Beman in designing virtually all the buildings in Pullman have earned these communities an important place in the textbooks. Less publicized but comparable in quality as military architecture are the older buildings and the original grounds of Fort Sheridan, although since private developers took over the base in the mid-1990s, the buildings they have constructed have been markedly inferior. During the first half of the twentieth century, some memorable ecclesiastical architecture was also put up in Chicago suburbs, none of it more spectacular than Louis Bourgeois's Baha'i House of Worship in Wilmette. The campus of Northwestern University in Evanston is the most important collective example of suburban architecture in the service of education, while Crow Island School in Winnetka by Eliel and Eero Saarinen with Perkins, Wheeler & Will has the distinction of representing a union of progressive educational philosophy and, for its time, progressive architectural form. Moreover, well before World War II, the suburbs had become sufficiently like the city in their activities and functions that their accomplishments in commercial and industrial buildings have been worthy of the company of their more renowned city relatives. In this category, the spectrum has extended from the patrician Lake Forest shopping center, Market Square, to the vernacular manner and monumental scale of the Western Electric factory in Cicero.

Nonetheless, the recent massive suburbanization has yielded its own new structural forms, which include, most obviously, shopping malls, industrial parks, planned communities, and tract housing. Most of these are clearly the spawn of the automobile, which has produced a landscape reflective of the ease of movement it possesses in greater degree than the railroad, past or present. Multilane expressways, visually striking examples of modern construction techniques especially at their points of intersection, have altered the whole metropolitan matrix while giving rise to commercial complexes strung along them in intervals too vast to be comprehended as communal in any traditional sense. Interstate 88 west of Chicago is a serviceable example. In addition, as developers turn profits by buying up farmlands at the exurban edge and converting them into housing tracts, the phenomenon commonly called urban sprawl is a natural consequence. And a controversial one: some observers have regarded such settlements affirmatively, arguing that they are less a genuinely new phenomenon and more a continuation, in contemporary technological terms, of a historical urban outward reach. Moreover, proponents contend that the new developments provide their inhabitants, especially younger families, the opportunity to leave the density of the city behind and to own their own homes, equipped with the front and backyards traditional to the American residential dream. Opponents point to the costs borne by somebody other than the developers: new infrastructure, schools and commercial services, and, above all, the increased burden of traffic congestion resulting from the heavier reliance on private automobiles and the unwillingness of car owners to endorse or to use public transportation. Yet in view of the greater distances from place to place that sprawl implies, it is hard to argue against the need for upgraded public transportation.

Meanwhile, yet another view of the automobile and its effect on architecture has grown out of a serious study of a genre of building that has sprung up along the roadsides—streets and highways alike—of modern America: motels, roadhouses, diners, service stations, as well as the signs that variously adorn them. It is not easy to identify individual works or even complexes that naturally belong to a book historically devoted to Chicago's famous buildings, but as a composite, these assorted districts warrant recognition, since they are clearly parts of a constructed and populated world that owes its existence and nature to the automobile.

At the same time, like a wind of great force from many directions, the decentralization caused by the automobile has produced eddies and swirls, new enterprises like the Oak Brook and Woodfield shopping malls, new towns like Elk Grove Village and Hoffman Estates, industrial parks like Baxter International Laboratories, even the "tract mansion" developments—gatherings of huge, expensive houses put up on cramped lots—that have mushroomed at and around the borders of established suburbs.

While the ultimate value of automobilia to society at large continues to be debated, any architectural study of Chicago or other American cities (increasingly those abroad as well) must make a place for it alongside the more conventional building forms that have also gone up during the last several generations throughout a metropolitan area that has not died—as the many doomsayers of the 1970s and 1980s predicted for the cities of the national northeast quadrant—but remained remarkably alive.

Old Orchard Center (1956)

Old Orchard Road and Skokie Boulevard, Skokie

ARCHITECTS: Loebl, Schlossman & Bennett

Perhaps more than any other product of contemporary popular culture, the shopping mall symbolizes the enormous growth of American suburbs since World War II and the impact of the automobile, which generated the growth.

The car has enabled whole populations not only to live and work well beyond the limits of the city, but to trade there as well, in wholly planned concentrations of retail outlets—the malls. Since they are usually built just far enough from population centers to still be reached easily by car, they have rendered main streets largely obsolete.

The most modest example of the new genre is the strip mall, where low storefronts are lined up in a long row behind vast parking lots. In the high-budget malls, on the other hand (e.g., Woodfield [155]), the shops

face inward to roofed corridors that run the length and width of what amounts to an introverted structure.

Old Orchard (a Westfield Shoppingtown) is a cross between the two types but different from either of them. The center is bordered by a parking area typical of malls, but its shops are organized in groups of buildings rather than in a single structure, with the spaces between given over to connecting pathways. Thus pedestrian traffic moves both indoors and outdoors.

[*142*] **Northwestern University: Evanston Campus** (1851–)
Sheridan Road between Clark and Lincoln Streets, Evanston

The most visually arresting passage on the university's Evanston campus is not a building. Rather it is the stretch of parkland that borders the campus's eastern edge, offering a spectacular, uninterrupted view of the lake. It extends from the bend in Sheridan Road on the south to Lincoln Street

on the north, almost a mile, longer than that of any other privately owned riparian space in the Chicago region.

Any walk along the shoreline is rewarding, especially since the university's 1961 decision to construct most of it on landfill has not only amplified the amount of green space but created a lagoon that separates most of the new land from the campus to the west, making for a pleasant relationship between land and water.

Founded in 1851, Northwestern had no master plan during its early years. In 1909 architect George W. Maher proposed such a scheme, in a formal, axial pattern, but the school never adopted it, and today most of the buildings are randomly sited on a campus much longer than it is wide.

The oldest surviving structure is the 1869 University Hall, a naive exercise in the Gothic mode that makes up in sentimental charm what it lacks in architectural sophistication. Succeeding decades saw the construction of a variety of buildings in assorted styles. The most notable of the older works is Deering Library (James Gamble Rogers, 1933), a collegiate Gothic exercise (based upon the sixteenth-century King's College Chapel at Cambridge University) that gains greatly from its siting at the rear of a splendid meadow bordering Sheridan Road. Indeed, landscaping is one of the best features of the Evanston campus, nowhere more so than in the wooded area around University Hall and in Shakespeare Garden, designed by Jens Jensen and located a few blocks north of Deering, in front of the Garrett-Evangelical Theological Seminary.

That said, it remains regrettable nonetheless that the university decided to place Leverone Hall and School of Education and Social Policy (Loebl, Schlossman, Bennett & Dart, 1972) so that it interrupts the expanse of Deering Meadow and breaks the crescent configuration of the older buildings facing toward it.

The university expanded greatly after 1955, and the buildings constructed meanwhile have followed modernist modes. One of the finest, the Lindheimer Astronomical Research Center (Skidmore, Owings & Merrill, 1966), was demolished in the mid-1990s. Skidmore, Owings & Merrill has also contributed a number of the respectable buildings that remain, including the Frances Searle Building (1972), the Seeley G. Mudd Library (1977), and the O. T. Hogan Biological Sciences Building (1967). Nonetheless, for resourcefulness of interior planning and boldness of exterior appearance, the University Library (1970), a trio of pavilions connected at the base to one another and to Deering, is Skidmore, Owings & Merrill's proudest campus accomplishment. (The lead designer was Walter Netsch.) Nearby are a group of very recent buildings, most notable among them the Arthur and Gladys Pancoe Evanston Northwestern Healthcare Life Sciences Pavilion (2003) and the Center for Nanofabrication and Molecular Self-Assembly (2002), both by Zimmer Gunsul Frasca. Along the northern limits of the campus, Holabird & Root is represented by two handsome athletic facilities, the Dellora A. and Lester J. Norris Aquatics Center and Henry Crown Sports Pavilion, both completed in 1987. The Combe Tennis Center, by Pollock Holzrichter Nicholas, was added to the Crown Pavilion in 2001. Meanwhile, a bit farther south, Perkins & Will was responsible for the Materials and Life Sciences Building (now called William A. and Gayle K. Cook Hall), and Booth Hansen Associates for Walter Annenberg Hall.

The most memorable structures on the southeast corner of the campus are Pick-Staiger Concert Hall (1975) by Loebl, Schlossman, Bennett & Dart; the Mary and Leigh Block Museum of Art (2000) by Lohan Associates; the McCormick Tribune Center (2002) by Einhorn Yoffee Prescott; and Mary Jane McMillen Crowe Hall (2002) by DeStefano & Partners.

West of the main campus, the university's football stadium, Ryan Field (formerly Dyche Stadium), was extensively renovated in 1996–97 by a team of architects and engineers led by Griskelis & Smith.

[*143*] **Baha'i House of Worship** (1953)
Sheridan Road at Linden Avenue, Wilmette
ARCHITECT: Louis Bourgeois

The Baha'i Temple, as it is commonly known, is one of the most visually arresting buildings on Chicago's North Shore. The public has long seen it that way, and while many architecture buffs have looked at it askance because its highly traditional appearance violates the precepts of orthodox modernism, even that negative opinion has softened as historicist design has begun to look better with the passing years. Begun in 1920,

construction was not completed until 1953. Money for the building was raised entirely by the temple congregants as their gift to the world's peoples.

The nine sides of the building stand for the largest single number, symbolic of the Baha'i belief in the unity and oneness of mankind. There is an equal number of entrances, each surmounted with a quotation from Bah'u'llah, founder of the faith. The temple is 191 feet high, with four stories of reinforced concrete, its surfaces alive with lacelike ornament, and the whole topped by a striking ribbed dome. Lake Michigan is visible from any seat in the auditorium, which is free of altars and images.

[*144*] **Crow Island School** (1940)

1112 Willow Road, Winnetka

ARCHITECTS: Eliel and Eero Saarinen; Perkins, Wheeler & Will

Winnetka has long prided itself on the quality of its elementary and secondary schools, and Crow Island School has only reinforced the village's well-deserved reputation. Since the building is executed in a perceptibly modernist manner, it is safe to say it stands for progressive architecture together with equally advanced concepts in education. That is evident enough in the design, in which the enhancement of the children's learning process was given high priority by the creation of an optimally comfortable physical environment. The single classroom was regarded as a module of sorts, each space emerging from a common hallway but kept cunningly separated from and united with its neighbor by an outdoor play area. The hallways make up three wings that extend outward from a central section given over to shared facilities. Warmth of color and texture was a conscious part of the building program, as were the charming

glazed ceramic sculptures that are set along the exterior walls. The innovative treatment of the Crow Island plan was a breakthrough that exercised considerable influence on the later design of schools.

[*145*] **North Shore Congregation Israel** (1964, 1983)
1185 Sheridan Road, Glencoe
ARCHITECTS: Minoru Yamasaki Associates (1964); addition, Hammond, Beeby & Babka (1983)

The largest component of this three-part building complex is the principal sanctuary, designed by Yamasaki so that its palpably organic appearance is achieved by an extraordinary structural system. The bays are joined by single continuous columnlike elements of reinforced concrete

that grow from slender stems at the base into leaflike cantilevers over-head. The bays on opposite sides of the interior join at the top to form the underside of the roof. In the space between the columns, the bays are filled by thin slabs of concrete bordered by amber glass and deco-rated on the exterior by a single delicate vertical concrete strip. Each end of the sanctuary is closed by yet another leaflike slab, with a central rib from which sets of veins emerge, curving downward and outward.

If the Yamasaki building is a strong example of his gracefully man-nered late modernist style, the addition by Hammond, Beeby & Babka conforms to the postmodernist taste of the early 1980s. From the out-side, its principal mass is a cleanly simplified brick cylinder with a portico featuring the Palladian motif. The main interior space, the Perlman Sanc-tuary, is effectively a cylinder within a cylinder. The decor is abundant with classical elements like round arches, oculi, and Tuscan Doric columns. A central axis leads to the Ark. Built to meet the congregation's need for a worship area smaller than the Yamasaki temple, the sanctuary leads through an east exit to the Rebecca K. Crown Social Hall, a large rectangular room from which a handsome view of Lake Michigan may be enjoyed.

[*146*] **Ward Willits House** (1902)
1445 Sheridan Road, Highland Park
ARCHITECT: Frank Lloyd Wright

Often called Wright's earliest authentic masterpiece, the Willits House is easily visible from Sheridan Road, just south of the business district of Highland Park. In many respects, it is a characteristic example of the ar-chitect's Prairie style, a name deriving largely from the horizontal sweep that is one of the Willits House's most impressive attributes. The living room, dining room, and service and reception areas radiate outward from a fireplace that serves as both the physical and spiritual center of the house. This open plan, a device further associated with Wright, is ap-parent in the almost uninterrupted flow of interior spaces. The influence of Japanese domestic architecture can be detected from the exterior, which is marked by light stucco surfaces enlivened by dark wood strips

and wide overhanging eaves. The multitude of leaded-glass windows is an especially attractive feature. Bedrooms on the second floor are similarly grouped around the core. A gardener's cottage also designed by Wright and later remodeled as a separate residence stands at the rear of the site.

[*147*] **Chicago Botanic Garden**
1000 Lake Cook Road, Glencoe

While the Chicago Horticultural Society was formally incorporated in 1890, the Chicago Botanic Garden did not materialize until the 1960s, when land was leased from the Cook County Forest Preserve, and the present splendid grounds were laid out in Glencoe, about twenty miles north of the city. Chicago and its environs can boast more than one example of superb landscape architecture, not least among them Frederick Law Olmsted's Jackson Park and Jens Jensen's Columbus Park, but the Botanic Garden compares favorably with the best of these, especially because it was designed as much to display beautiful and varied botanical specimens as to provide parkland space for visitors.

The people are legion who have enjoyed to the fullest the Botanic Garden's offerings, which include buildings as surely as plantings. Located on islands within and along the edges of lagoons bordering the Skokie River, the grounds are readily accessible year-round. Although most of the landscape has been shaped and kept up by the Pittsburgh firm of Environment Planning and Design, several individual components have had their own designers: chiefly the Japanese Garden, by Koichi Kawana; the Herb Garden, by Janet Meakin Poor; the English Walled Garden, by John Brookes; and the East and West Courtyards of the Garden's Education Center, by Franz Lipp.

The three principal structures are products of New York architect Edward Larrabee Barnes. The Education Center (1976) and the Gateway Visitor Center (1993) are four-square prisms built of a handsome beige-orange brick, each surmounted by a hipped roof and topped by a cupola cunningly constructed to admit light to the interior below. The Education Center is attached to group of greenhouses, and the Gateway Visitor Center is served by a restaurant. Another refectory is part of Barnes's third building, the McGinley Pavilion.

The sixty-foot Butz Memorial carillon tower designed by I. P. Berdin of Cincinnati and located on Evening Island features forty-eight bronze bells ranging from twenty-four pounds to two and a half tons. An assortment of public sculptures is arranged throughout the grounds, most notably Robert Berks's super-life-sized bronze portrait of Carolus Linnaeus, the eighteenth-century Swedish botanist who founded the system of modern taxonomy.

Fort Sheridan Historic District (1888–91)

Main entrance: Sheridan Road at Old Elm Road, between Highland
Park and Lake Forest

ARCHITECTS: Holabird & Roche

LANDSCAPE ARCHITECT: Ossian C. Simonds

Isolated voluntarily by its military mission and involuntarily by the exclu-
sivity of its elegant neighbors, Lake Forest and Highland Park, Fort Sheridan is one of the best-kept secrets of the North Shore. Yet in the unity of
its buildings styles, its planning, and its distribution of functions, it quali-
fies as one of the most successful urban accomplishments in the metropolitan area.

The main entrance leads on an east-west axis to a large parade
ground, designed by Ossian Simonds, that also serves as a mall. Its domi-

nant feature is a lofty and dignified formal watchtower, the most imposing of the many buildings erected by Holabird & Roche in the fort's historical district. The common yellow brick used throughout the post lends a plain but impressive consistency to the styles—chiefly Queen Anne, neo-Romanesque, and vernacular variations—of the administrative buildings, depots, shops, drill buildings, and housing units. Especially noteworthy are the three looping lanes of officers' houses radiating from the mall eastward toward the lake. Embellished by handsome stands of oaks and maples and separated by generous expanses of lawn, the houses are mostly gabled prisms with arched porches and occasional turret corners.

With the end of the Cold War and reductions in the national defense budget, Fort Sheridan joined many military facilities in search of a new use. After a military support center was established in 1993 on a small portion of the site, the possibilities for redeveloping a large parcel of land along Lake Michigan attracted great interest. In the debate regarding the best use for the soon-to-be-former fort, citizens sought to balance public values and private ambitions. So far, they have failed. No large public park has been developed. The quality of the conversion and rehabilitation of existing fort buildings ranges from tolerable to questionable to thoughtless. New buildings erected so far are routinely deplorable. Despite the quality of the new work, enough of the character of the original fort and grounds remains to appreciate the original intent.

[*149*] **Lake Forest**

Although settled as early as the 1830s, Lake Forest did not begin to take on the character of a community until after wealthy Chicago Presbyterians purchased land in a heavily wooded area of the city's North Shore and turned it into a planned town equipped with an institution of higher learning. Financial reverses delayed the founding of the school later known as Lake Forest University and finally as Lake Forest College, but by the 1870s the village was widely accepted throughout the Chicago area as the most socially prestigious of the city's suburbs.

The first notable design achievement was the town plan of 1857, now certainly attributed to Almerin Hotchkiss, a surveyor and planner associ-

LAKE FOREST and its SCHOOLS
1868

SCALE
30 CHAINS TO THE INCH

ated with St. Louis. An informal network of curving roads repeating and sometimes following the contours of the ravines that wind down to the lake, the plat is an outgrowth of the romantic tradition and traceable to eighteenth-century English gardens, early-nineteenth-century American communal cemeteries and parks, and the theories of naturalistic landscaping promoted in America by Andrew Jackson Downing. Hotchkiss's plan preceded Frederick Law Olmsted's more famous layout of Riverside (164) by at least a decade. It also encouraged the early rusticity of Lake Forest as well as the town's reputation for leisurely, untrammeled society.

The opening of the Onwentsia Country Club in 1893 was instrumental in prompting members of Chicago's best-known families, including the McCormicks, the Swifts, and the Armours, to build homes in an increasingly urbane Lake Forest. Slowly the local custom of summer residence gave way to year-round living. Thus the town's business center, Market Square, as well as its numerous grand mansions, were built after the turn of the twentieth century.

The show of wealth traditionally associated with Lake Forest is still strikingly evident, most prominently in the estates along Lake Road and Green Bay Road, many of which were designed by Howard Van Doren Shaw and David Adler.

[**150**] **Market Square** (1916)
700 North Western Avenue, Lake Forest
ARCHITECT: Howard Van Doren Shaw

Certifiably one of the oldest planned shopping centers in the nation, Market Square is a charming congeries of traditional styles, its gabled, Tudor half-timbered fronts (with offices upstairs and shops downstairs) in easy accord with the classicism of the Marshall Field store and the northern European eclecticism of the two towers flanking the entrance to the area. The detailing in several of the buildings reflects Shaw's personal devotion to the international Arts and Crafts movement.

1230 North Green Bay Road, Lake Forest
ARCHITECT: Howard Van Doren Shaw

Shaw designed more than thirty private homes in Lake Forest, several of them more imposing but none more ingratiating than his own residence. Ragdale's indebtedness to the Arts and Crafts movement is apparent both inside and out. The white stucco surfaces of the house are appropriate to its modest dimensions. The front facade, crowned by a pair of gables, features windows with flower boxes and a vine-covered loggia. The choice interior space is the dining room, visible from the entry hall through two window screens studded with diamond-shaped panes. The Ragdale estate as a whole is notable on several accounts. One of the outbuildings is a remodeled barn dating from the 1840s, faintly Greek Revival in profile and the oldest standing structure in Lake Forest. Sixteen acres sloping gently to the west include stretches of virgin prairie.

Now owned by the city of Lake Forest, the property is the home of the Ragdale Foundation, the most important artists' community in the Midwest.

[*152*] **Mrs. Kersey Coates Reed House** (1930)

1315 Lake Road, Lake Forest

ARCHITECT: David Adler

One of the great American society architects of the twentieth century, David Adler left a substantial number of his most memorable works in Lake Forest. He was an eclectic by habit and preference, drawing almost omnivorously on a wide variety of historical manners and combining them in felicitous stylistic marriages. The Reed House owes something to the plan of Palladian villas in its main tract with symmetrically extending arms, while the Georgian facade is clad in gray Pennsylvania mica stone. The interior is notable for a dramatic entry gallery that ends in an elegant curving staircase adorned with spare classical motifs. A mirrored powder room and a leather-lined library are among other arresting features.

[*153*] **Crabtree Farm**

Sheridan Road, immediately north of Lake Bluff

ARCHITECT: Solon S. Beman

Located on the north edge of the village of Lake Bluff, Crabtree Farm encompasses the land between Sheridan Road and Lake Michigan. Since it is privately owned, the only portion the public can see is the group of

buildings visible from Sheridan Road. Nevertheless, these are close enough to capture and reward the viewer's attention. The original owner was Mrs. Scott Durand, who conceived and operated it as a dairy farm before moving its operations from Lake Forest to Lake Bluff in 1906, whereupon she commissioned Solon S. Beman to design the buildings as they now stand. The current owner has converted much of the farm to other uses.

Beman's composition consists of two sets of adjacent gabled buildings, topped with small cupolas, that face each other across a sunken forecourt, as a fifth and larger structure, adorned with a clock tower and belfry, dominates the group, generating an overall U-shaped plan. The smaller buildings are clad in stucco and roofed in precast concrete made to look like tile. One of the north pair has been turned into a lodge, and its counterpart on the south into a house that is now called Stickley Cottage. The towered structure remains a barn. The interiors of the furnished buildings are filled with furniture and decorative arts by Gustav Stickley and his contemporaries. Nearer Sheridan Road are two structures similarly outfitted. The so-called Harvey Ellis House, on the north, was built in the early 1990s after an Ellis plan that had been originally published in a 1902 edition of *The Craftsman* magazine. The old well house on the south edge has been made over in imitation of Gustav Stickley's office.

Baxter International Laboratories (1975)

One Baxter Parkway, Deerfield

ARCHITECTS: Skidmore, Owings & Merrill

The steady recent expansion, indeed the urbanization, of the Chicago suburban network has led more than a few major industries to move their plants and headquarters to sites outside the city. Among the most architecturally noteworthy is the Baxter International Laboratories group near Deerfield, seen most readily and comprehensively from the Tri-State Tollway. Four steel-framed pavilions surround the Central Facilities Building, which is the dominant element in the complex in size, structural inventiveness, and overall visual impact. The roof is hung on cables suspended in turn from two powerful columns rising thirty-five feet above roof level. More cables on the underside of the roof, fixed to the columns and extending upward from them, help to stiffen the roof.

The upper system of cables is visible from the outside, while the lower is equally apparent from within the great cafeteria space that takes up most of the upper level. (The lower level is given over to a training school, an auditorium, a reception area, and an executive dining room.) The facade of the building is an imposing wall of glass, 288 feet long, 48 feet high, and detailed in white-painted aluminum.

[**155**] **Woodfield Shopping Center** (1971)

5 Woodfield Shopping Center, Golf Road and Route 53, Schaumburg

ARCHITECTS: Jickling & Lyman

There seems no end in sight to the spread of suburban shopping malls and the gargantuan business districts to which they are symbiotically connected. When Woodfield opened in 1971, it was the largest indoor mall in the world, a superlative it has long since lost to more than a few global rivals. Even so, it remains so large that its dimensions cannot be easily taken in by its patrons, who can scarcely make their way to its entrance except by automobile. The exterior can be perceived in full only from the air, while internally the axes of its four arms are intentionally set ajog where they meet in the immense central court, thus insuring that no vista is too long to discourage a shopper from exploring its full length. The stupendous surrounding acreage—given over to office buildings, motion picture theater complexes, superhighways, viaducts, and even other malls—is a signal that the area has been a palpable popular and economic success, as definitive a measure of the contemporary architectural landscape as any visitor from Mars might discover.

Little differentiates the plans of Oak Park and its neighbor River Forest from that of Chicago. Both suburbs are laid out on the grid that is standard throughout the American Midwest as a whole and Chicago specifically. Indeed the opposite of Oak Park and River Forest within the greater metropolitan area must be Lake Forest and Riverside, each of which was conceived by an identifiable individual as an informal web of picturesquely winding roads, moreover as a perceptibly delimited community. Thus Oak Park and River Forest, in effect extensions of the Chicago street pattern, are more nearly suburbs in the exact sense of the word, while Lake Forest and Riverside in their containment may be more properly regarded as exurban creations. Consequently, there must be a different reason for assigning Oak Park a special place in the annals of Chicago architecture. His name is Frank Lloyd Wright. A resident of Oak Park from 1889 to 1909, Wright not only left a rich legacy of buildings there but attracted a coterie of followers who made up what is commonly called the Prairie school.

More important, Wright drew from the tableland west of Chicago the inspiration to produce a uniquely American residential architecture. In the outward reach of its horizontal exterior forms and the openness of its interior plans, it reflected the seemingly endless and multidirectional expansion of the prairie. No understanding of Wright and his singular contribution to international architecture can be understood without an awareness of the dozens of houses he and his disciples left in Oak Park and River Forest.

[*157*] Forest Avenue
Between Chicago Avenue and Ontario Street, Oak Park

Oak Park is internationally renowned, mostly because of the imprint left there by Frank Lloyd Wright and his Prairie school followers, chief among them George W. Maher, Thomas Tallmadge, John S. Van Bergen, and Vernon Spencer Watson.

Wright's work in Oak Park is most concentrated along the tree-lined stretch of Forest Avenue from Chicago Avenue south to Ontario Street. Seven of the houses on the street are by him, although most visitors make it a point to examine an eighth, the house of Mrs. Thomas H. Gale at 6 Elizabeth Court, a cul-de-sac that jogs off Forest about halfway along the route. Wright's earliest expressive manner is visible in the shingle-style treatment of his own home (1889; 158), while one of the most ma-

ture achievements is the Gale House (1909; 159), the hard geometries of which prefigure European modernism of the 1920s.

Stylistically, these two houses bracket a wide array of types. The William H. Copeland House (at 400), put up by another builder in 1873, was remodeled in 1908–9 by Wright, who added his most typical touches to the interior spaces. The Edward R. Hills House (at 313), dating from 1874, is also a remodeling (in 1906), but there Wright's hand was exercised thoroughly throughout, though the sloping rooflines are, for him, curiously *retardataire*. The gables that dominate the Peter A. Beachy House (at 238 [1906]) and Nathan G. Moore House (at 333 [1895, reconstructed by Wright in 1923 after a fire]) are similarly uncharacteristic; indeed the openly derivative English Tudor features of the Moore House testify to Wright's occasional willingness to accommodate himself to a client's tastes. But in the low, wide eaves and ribbon casements of the Arthur Heurtley House (at 318 [1902]) and the all-stucco facade of the Frank W. Thomas House (at 210 [1901]), Wright was his own man, in command of the principles and devices that marked the fully articulated Prairie style.

[*158*] **Frank Lloyd Wright Home and Studio** (1889–98)
951 Chicago Avenue, Oak Park
ARCHITECT: Frank Lloyd Wright

The learning laboratory for the first two decades of his career, the dwelling and studio Wright designed for himself and his family has been carefully restored to its appearance in 1909, the year he left his family. Begun in 1889, when he was twenty-two, with a loan from his employer Louis Sullivan, the small house grew with the expansion of the dining room and creation of the children's playroom in 1895. He added the studio in 1898. The simple gabled initial house incorporated elements of the

popular shingle style and Colonial Revival. The enlarged dining room exploited newly available electric light, horizontality, and the concept of the room within a room. The children's playroom investigated the barrel vault in contrast with transverse windows, as well as false perspective in the balcony that extended into former attic space. The implied polygons he explored in the living-room bay windows were fully investigated in the studio, where an octagon rested on a square in the studio and an octagon was rotated again and again in the library. Throughout, Wright matched formal manipulation with a desire to discover the possibilities of color, art glass, cast materials, and surface texture.

In 1974 the National Trust for Historic Preservation acquired the complex. The Frank Lloyd Wright Home and Studio Foundation (renamed in 2000 as the Frank Lloyd Wright Preservation Trust) was founded as the local operating entity. The foundation secured and restored the building, and the National Trust provided oversight. Many of the surviving pieces of furniture Wright designed for the building have been returned through gift or acquisition, as well as some decorative art that Wright collected when he lived there.

6 Elizabeth Court, Oak Park

ARCHITECT: Frank Lloyd Wright

A marvelous surprise, hidden beyond a curve and tucked among traditional houses on a tight site, Wright's house for Laura Gale summarizes his roots in the nineteenth century and his ambitions for the twentieth. The central fireplace core, to which he returned frequently, is rooted in the traditional American past, while the cantilevered trays of the porches, framed by ambiguous piers, ribbon windows, and hovering roof, indicate the agenda he would explore for the next half-century. Constructed in 1909, it may have been designed as early as 1904, before Thomas Gale died in 1907. While the ample windows and projecting porches imply that the house is open and transparent, Wright lifted the house just enough above the site to provide visual privacy to occupants seated in either the living room or on its porch. Occupants of the porch have the pleasure of being unobserved behind the parapet while overhearing the remarks of sightseers standing only a few feet away on the street

[**160**] **Unity Temple** (1906)
(Unitarian Universalist Church)
875 Lake Street at Kenilworth Avenue, Oak Park
ARCHITECT: Frank Lloyd Wright

Wright made a great advance with this building in terms of its form, structure, and purpose. Best known as an architect of houses, Wright designed Unity Temple as a public building for a noble purpose. Well known for how lightly his buildings could touch the ground, the reinforced-concrete structure of Unity Temple clearly expresses its massive weight. Famous for his ability to destroy the box, in Unity Temple Wright celebrates the box.

Public buildings usually address the street, as does the newer church across Lake Street. Wright turned this approach inside out, presenting the largely opaque volume of the sanctuary to the street, and thereby forcing the visitor to walk along the building's sheer mass to discover the nearly transparent entrance. Upon climbing the entry stairs, one sees a glazed series of doors that apparently lead straight out to the glazed doors on the other side of the building. The motto over the door—"For the worship of God and the service of man"—describes the choices encountered on entering the building. To one side is the parish house/service space, visually accessible through two large passages/doors. To the other side is a solid, opaque wall plane, with passages to the sides that require going down or up stairs and taking multiple turnings until finally arriving, usually after a series of screened glimpses, in the great centralized space. The multiple paths to the pews and the distanced quality of the visually separate main level and the surrounding spaces reinforce the clarity of the concept of, and the complexity of the search for, unity.

Concrete was well known throughout the nineteenth century as a useful and inexpensive industrial material, but few architects had attempted to exploit the material as an expressive element. Wright suggested the appropriateness of the material by washing the surface of the raw concrete to reveal its pebble aggregate.

Wright exploited the prevailing view of concrete as a heavy and massive element in his forms for the building. One's initial view of the building suggests a monolith, but careful regard shows the building to be formed of many cubic and planar masses separated by both thin and thick zones of art glass. This separation is most marked in the interior. Some of the masses appear to be insubstantial, as Wright bends wooden striping around corners. The weighty roof plane seems to float on a cushion of light if seen from the outside at night or from the inside on a sunny day.

A restoration program began in 1969 and was formalized with the 1973 creation of the Unity Temple Restoration Foundation, which continues to pursue its goal. The exterior walls have been renewed using aggregate from the same quarry as originally. The lay-lights and skylights of the sanctuary have been restored, while the cantilevered eaves of the roof have yet to be done. The interior colors have been analyzed and restored. The restoration program will be completed in 2008.

[*161*] **Pleasant Home** (1897)

(John Farson House)

217 Home Avenue, Oak Park

ARCHITECT: George W. Maher

This ambitious design by Maher declares his allegiance to the ideas of broadness of conception and simplification of mass and surface encouraged by Richardson at the Glessner House (1887; 123) and accomplished by Wright in the Winslow House (1894; 162). The stolid horizontality of the house, with chiseled openings and smooth surfaces, and the expanse of the parklike site declare this a house of great presence and assurance. The broadness of the exterior is continued on the interior, enriched and enlivened by the use of exotic wood, tile work, art glass, and metal. Since it is now owned by the village of Oak Park, plans have been made to develop the building as a house museum. The collections of the Historical Society of Oak Park and River Forest are also displayed in the building.

[*162*] **Winslow House** (1894)

515 Auvergne Place, River Forest

ARCHITECT: Frank Lloyd Wright

Wright's design for William Winslow is significant in several ways. Wright created for Winslow, a manufacturer of ornamental iron products, the dwelling that announces the architect's gifts and the importance of sym-

pathetic clients. The main block of the house is rigidly symmetric and reserved. However, the porte cochere pulls that order off center, and this is further questioned by the stable at the back of the site. If seen from Edgewood Place, the jumpy asymmetrical verticality of the rear elevation of the house declares that all has not been resolved. In his *Autobiography*, Wright described the Winslow House as his first independent commission. The plan, too, is suggestive if unclear. The handling of the masonry and planarity of the front elevation is indebted to Wright's apprenticeship in Sullivan's office—for instance, his involvement with the Charnley House (90). When first constructed, the plaster frieze that forms the wall of the second floor was painted a light tan. This caused viewers to have a far stronger sense that the deeply overhanging roof was floating above the house on a cushion of light. This created the effect that the three major elements of the house—enclosing masonry wall, floating roof, and central chimney stack—described the idea of shelter in the most elemental manner possible. This was also the location of the Auvergne Press, where Wright and Winslow designed, illustrated, and printed in 1897 an elegant edition of William Gannett's *The House Beautiful*.

[*163*] **Drummond House** (1909)
559 Edgewood Place, River Forest
ARCHITECT: William B. Drummond
Roberts House (1908)
603 Edgewood Place, River Forest
ARCHITECT: Frank Lloyd Wright

Drummond designed and built this house for himself and his wife after spending most of the prior ten years in Frank Lloyd Wright's office. The projecting front porch, hovering roof, strip windows, and interpenetrating planes declare his mastery of the idiom of the Prairie school and his interest in extending its possibilities. The first-floor plan explores space that is suggestive if not fully resolved. Like many other Prairie houses, Drummond designed for concrete, but costs forced him to realize the building with stucco on a wooden frame. Originally, the visible wooden framing and decorative elements were stained in brown slightly darker than the stucco.

The house Wright designed for Isabel Roberts, his office manager, is an early example of a dwelling entered just above grade. The large public space of the house faces the street, while private sleeping spaces on the upper level face the backyard. Although subsequently enclosed, the

open porch to the right of the front of the house included a tree accommodated through its roof.

Taken together, these two dwellings suggest how well the Prairie mode could deal with the conventions of the design of residential districts in small towns, big cities, and, as here, suburbs.

[*164*] **Riverside** (1869)

PLANNER: Frederick Law Olmsted

Enough remains of the original plan and the early buildings of Riverside to secure the community's long-standing reputation as one of the handsomest in the Chicago area. The plat dates from 1869, when Frederick Law Olmsted, the most illustrious American landscape architect of his day, laid out Riverside in a pattern of curving streets disposed on both sides of parkland bordering the Des Plaines River. Inspired by the romantic and to a degree "antimodern" belief in a townscape free of the presumed constraints and artificiality of the conventional grid, Olmsted wrote of his intention at Riverside: "As the ordinary directness of line in town streets, with its resultant regularity of plan[,] would suggest eagerness to press forward . . . we would recommend . . . gracefully curved lines, generous spaces, and the absence of sharp corners, the idea

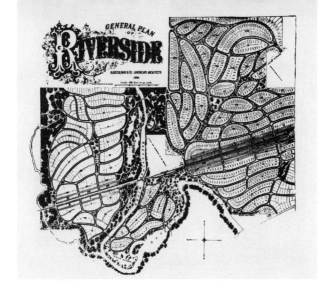

being to suggest and imply leisure, contemplativeness and happy tranquility."

Even so, it is worth recalling that Olmsted designed Riverside not as a resort remote from Chicago, but as a town dependent on the city and its connecting railroad. Moreover, he imposed controls of his own on the village, including standard lots of 100 by 225 feet and the requirement that houses be set back 30 feet from the street. Many splendid old residences enliven the sweeping, tree-lined drives produced by this plan. The center of town is still distinguished by its historic buildings, notably the Chicago, Burlington & Quincy railroad station, its adjacent 108-foot water tower, and an office building executed in the Victorian Gothic manner.

[*165*] **Coonley Complex** (1907, 1911, 1912)
300 Scottswood, Riverside
ARCHITECT: Frank Lloyd Wright
Coonley Playhouse (1912)
350 Fairbank Road, Riverside
ARCHITECT: Frank Lloyd Wright

The complex of buildings Frank Lloyd Wright designed for Avery and Queene Ferry Coonley and the related landscape were among his largest

domestic commissions and show Wright in the full confidence of his powers. The very large principal dwelling was designed in 1907 and has since been divided into two units. Designed in 1911, both a gardener's cottage and a garage and stable (now called the coach house) are now dwellings. The sequence of lawns and courts formed by these buildings, set near the inner point of a sharp oxbow in the nearby Des Plaines River, creates a series of interrelated spaces similar to the richness and variety of Wright's interiors. The hovering hipped roofs, wood frame and stucco wall planes, and tile and art-glass surfaces of the building combine to define the masses. The subtle color palette helps lead from the site into the varied plans of the interiors, where the principal rooms, as at the Robie House, are one level above grade.

The Coonley Playhouse is on a separate site from the rest of the complex. This small building is monumental in form and intimate in scale. It combines the implied order of a symmetric, cruciform plan with a relaxed and seemingly accidental circulation. The interpenetration of mass and plane are expressed in both the solidity of the enclosing stucco walls and the translucent and transparent parade of balloons and flags in the art-glass windows.

[*166*] **St. Procopius Benedictine Abbey** (1970)
5601 College Road, Lisle
ARCHITECTS: Loebl, Schlossman, Bennett & Dart

Edward Dart worked closely with members of the abbey to achieve a place fit for monastic life that demonstrated his ideas about material, light, and space. From the founder of the order to present times, Bene-

dictines have often sought and secured distinguished architecture. The abbeys at Monte Cassino (destroyed in World War II) and Monte Oliveto Maggiore in Italy and at Melk in Austria are important examples of this tradition. Although not a Benedictine, Procopius did serve the Czechs, the community this abbey served in Chicago's eponymous Pilsen neighborhood in the nineteenth century. When the members of St. Procopius had saved enough money to build their first permanent home, they presented Dart with a site on a slight rise in a gently rolling landscape. Dart organized the abbey so that the church was at the top and the other, smaller elements stepped down the slope. One enters along a path around the exterior of the church, which offers unfolding views between walls of Chicago's tan and pink common brick, of Richard Hunt's sculpture of St. Procopius, of the bell tower, and finally of the compressed entry. Once inside, the path is directed by light falling over walls of the same common brick. Dart compared this spiraling path and organization of the monastery to the continuous curve of the volute of an Ionic capital. The end of the spiral—the altar of the church—is balanced by the array of choice and complexity Dart introduced into the other components of the plan. While one path may be favored, many paths can be followed. Paths leading in are different from paths leading out. For a community of long-term residents, this range of paths and variety of light means that the architecture is always offering new views of familiar elements.

[*167*] **Farnsworth House** (1946–51)
River Road east of Ben Street, Plano
ARCHITECT: Ludwig Mies van der Rohe

The Farnsworth House is one of Mies van der Rohe's three completed residential designs in the United States, and by far the most celebrated. It is also Mies's first realized example of a unitary space enclosed in a rectangular prism, a building form that more than any other distinguishes his American work from his European.

The house is a remarkable distillate of structure and space: a floor slab and a roof slab are welded to eight wide-flange columns, four to a side, that have been sandblasted to a smooth surface and painted white.

The exterior walls are panes of floor-to-ceiling glass hung behind—that is to say, within—the enclosing columns. The slabs are cantilevered from the column rows so that on the western, short side they form an entry deck accessible by a flowing stair from an asymmetrically oriented terrace, itself reached by another low stair from ground level.

The house is located near the edge of the Fox River near Plano (about fifty miles southwest of Chicago). Thus it sits on a flood plain, a fact that prompted Mies to raise the floor slab about five feet above the ground. That functional motive is perceptibly matched by an aesthetic consideration, since the whiteness of the steel and the transparency of the glass give the structure a floating, near-apparitional effect.

The interior, organized around a core veneered in primavera, contains a kitchen, storage, two bathrooms, and a fireplace. There is also a freestanding teak closet nearby. So disposed, these elements suggest, without defining, sitting, dining, sleeping, and kitchen areas, all linked by unpartitioned space. The house was commissioned as a country retreat for a single person, Dr. Edith Farnsworth, a Chicago physician.

British developer Peter Palumbo purchased the house from Dr. Farnsworth in 1972, and hired the landscape architect Lanning Roper to give the grounds the informal quality of an English garden. He also saw

to the full restoration of the house following a catastrophic flood in 1996, when water rose to a level about five feet above the floor.

The 1996 flood and one that followed the next year have persuaded some observers to place blame for the height of the water on the increased amount of built settlements in the Plano area. With so many new houses, driveways, and streets added to the country nearby, a phenomenon reflective of the sprawl that is currently creeping ever farther out from the city, some of the water that would have found drainage a generation ago has no runoff space today. The consequence is an increased likelihood of flooding throughout the surrounding area.

[*168*] **Ford House** (1949)
404 South Edgelawn, Aurora
ARCHITECT: Bruce Goff

The reputation of Bruce Goff, whose approach to building was highly original if not idiosyncratic, has profited greatly from a recent change in taste that has granted increased attention to alternatives to International Style modernism. One of his works that has contributed to this shift is the Ford House, exceptional in its open, two-level, circular plan and its use of exotic materials, including marine rope, coal, copper, cypress, and even metal ribbing from a World War II Quonset hut. To identify the house

as a building with a centralized plan and two symmetrical wings is to make it seem unremarkable. To describe it as a pumpkin-shaped residence with rocklike chunks of glass set in the walls to admit light is to suggest a mere curiosity. While both descriptions are accurate, neither conveys the potent originality of Goff's vision.

The Ghost City

This book is celebratory in nature. We recognize the great riches of our buildings, and we congratulate ourselves on their enduring presence, which contributes so much to the character of this great city. Yet since this book first appeared, many of its selections have been destroyed, usually by the enormous forces and pressures of development in the center of large cities.

This list of demolished buildings is highly selective, in no way encyclopedic or exhaustive. It could be expanded, but we hope it fairly represents the range of wounds that Chicago has inflicted on itself. Indifference and neglect are as significant to the failures of preservation as are care, innovation, and vigilance to its successes.

So here we remind readers as well as ourselves of the losses we have suffered. Buildings cannot be consigned to storage—the way books and paintings that go out of fashion can be—while waiting for tastes to change. We believe that buildings are gifts from the past held in trust for the future. We desire that our successors recognize us for our discernment rather than our destructiveness.

Recently a building was turned down for landmark designation, in part because it had not been included in this book. While buildings discussed here are among the most significant in Chicago, it is wrong to conclude that a building is without significance because it has not been included.

The following buildings never appeared in prior editions:

Midway Gardens (1914–1929)
ARCHITECT: Frank Lloyd Wright

Marshall Field Wholesale Store (1885–1930)
Block bounded by Adams, Wells, Quincy, and Franklin Streets
ARCHITECT: H. H. Richardson

Mecca Flats (1891–1952)
3350 South Michigan Avenue
ARCHITECTS: Willoughby J. Edbrooke and Franklin Pierce Burnham

Walker Warehouse (1888–1953)
ARCHITECTS: Adler & Sullivan

Republic Building (1905–1961)
201–209 South State Street
ARCHITECTS: Holabird & Roche

Federal Building (1905–1965/66)
Block bounded by Clark Street, Adams Street, Dearborn Street, and Jackson Boulevard
ARCHITECT: Henry Ives Cobb

Italian Court (1921–1969)
ARCHITECT: Robert de Golyer

Michigan Square Building (1930–1973)

Diana Court, North Michigan Avenue

ARCHITECTS: Holabird & Root

This group includes those buildings listed in earlier editions of this book:

Schiller Building/Garrick Theater (1892–1961)

64 West Randolph Street

ARCHITECTS: Adler & Sullivan

Cable Building (1899–1961)

57 East Jackson Boulevard

ARCHITECTS: Holabird & Roche

Lind Block (1852–1963)

Wacker Drive and Randolph Street

ARCHITECT: unknown

Hammond Library, Union Theological Seminary

(1882–1963)

Ashland Avenue and Warren Boulevard

ARCHITECTS: Adler & Sullivan

First Infantry Armory (1890–1966)

Michigan Avenue and Sixteenth Street

ARCHITECTS: Burnham & Root

Meyer Building (1892–1967)

307 West Van Buren Street

ARCHITECTS: Adler & Sullivan

Francis Apartments (1895–1967)

4304 South Forestville Avenue

ARCHITECT: Frank Lloyd Wright

Edison Shop (1912–1967)

229 South Wabash Avenue

ARCHITECTS: Purcell, Feick & Elmslie

Yondorf Building (1874–1968)

225–229 South Wacker Drive

ARCHITECT: unknown

Giles Building (1875–1968)

423–429 South Wabash Avenue

ARCHITECT: Otis L. Wheelock

Sullivan House (1892–1970)

4575 South Lake Park

ARCHITECTS: Adler & Sullivan

Hiram Sibley Warehouse (1882–1971)

315–331 North Clark Street

ARCHITECT: George H. Edbrooke

Grand Central Station (1890–1971)

Harrison and Wells Streets

ARCHITECT: Solon S. Beman

First Leiter Building (1879–1972)

208 West Monroe Street

ARCHITECT: William Le Baron Jenney

Chicago Stock Exchange (1894–1972)

30 North LaSalle Street

ARCHITECTS: Adler & Sullivan

Francisco Terrace Apartments (1895–1974)

253–257 North Francisco Avenue

ARCHITECT: Frank Lloyd Wright

Hunter Building (1908–1978)

(Later Liberty Mutual Insurance Building)

337 West Madison Street

ARCHITECT: Christian A. Eckstorm

The Coliseum (1900–1982)

1513 South Wabash Avenue

ARCHITECTS: Frost & Granger

ENGINEERS: E. C. & R. M. Shankland

Chicago and North Western Station (1911–1984)

West Madison Street at Canal Street

ARCHITECTS: Frost & Granger

McCarthy Building (1872–1990)

32 West Washington Street

ARCHITECT: John Mills van Osdel

United States Gypsum Building (1963–1994)

101 South Wacker Drive

ARCHITECTS: Perkins & Will

Chicago Stadium (1929–1995)

1800 West Madison Street

ARCHITECTS: Hall, Lawrence & Ratcliffe

Bibliography

Abernathy, Ann, and John G. Thorpe. *The Oak Park Home and Studio of Frank Lloyd Wright.* Oak Park, Ill.: Frank Lloyd Wright Home and Studio Foundation, 1988.

Algren, Nelson. *City on the Make.* Chicago: University of Chicago Press, 2001.

Alofsin, Anthony, *Frank Lloyd Wright—the Lost Years 1910–1922: A Study in Influence.* Chicago: University of Chicago Press, 1993.

Andreas, A. T. *History of Chicago: From the Earliest Period to the Present Time.* 3 vols. Chicago, 1884–86.

Art Institute of Chicago. "The Architecture of the Art Institute of Chicago." *Museum Studies* 14, no. 1 (1988).

———. *Architecture in Context: 360 North Michigan Avenue, the London Guaranty and Accident Company Building, the Stone Container Building.* Chicago: Art Institute of Chicago, 1981.

———. *Chicago Architects Design: A Century of Architectural Drawings from the Art Institute of Chicago.* Chicago: Art Institute of Chicago, 1982.

———. *The Plan of Chicago, 1909–1979.* Chicago: Art Institute of Chicago, 1979.

Bach, Ira J., and Mary Lackritz Gray. *A Guide to Chicago's Public Sculpture.* Chicago: University of Chicago Press, 1983.

Bachrach, Julia. *The City in a Garden: A Photographic History of Chicago's Parks*. Chicago: University of Chicago Press, 2001.

Berger, Philip, ed. *Highland Park: American Suburb at Its Best: An Architectural and Historical Survey.* Highland Park, Ill.: Highland Park Landmark Preservation Committee, 1982.

Bigott, Joseph C. *From Cottage to Bungalow: Houses and the Working Class in Metropolitan Chicago, 1869–1929.* Chicago: University of Chicago Press, 2001.

Block, Jean F. *Hyde Park Houses: An Informal History, 1856–1910.* Chicago: University of Chicago Press, 1978.

————. *The Uses of Gothic: Planning and Building the Campus of the University of Chicago, 1882–1932.* Chicago: University of Chicago Library, 1983.

Bluestone, Daniel M. *Constructing Chicago.* New Haven: Yale University Press, 1991.

Brooks, Gwendolyn. *In the Mecca; Poems*. New York: HarperCollins, 1968.

Brooks, H. Allen. *The Prairie School: Frank Lloyd Wright and His Midwest Contemporaries.* Toronto: University of Toronto Press, 1973.

Bruegmann, Robert. *The Architects and the City: Holabird & Roche of Chicago, 1880–1918.* Chicago: University of Chicago Press, 1997.

————. *Holabird & Roche and Holabird & Root: An Illustrated Catalog of Works, 1880–1940.* New York: Garland, 1991.

Buder, Stanley. *Pullman: An Experiment in Industrial Order and Community Planning, 1880–1930.* New York: Oxford University Press, 1967.

Burnham, Daniel H., and Edward H. Bennett. *Plan of Chicago* (1909; facsimile ed.) New York: Princeton Architectural Press, 1993.

Cahan, Richard. *The All Fall Down: Richard Nickel's Struggle to Save America's Architecture*. Hoboken: John Wiley, 1994.

Casari, Maurizio, and Vincenzo Pavan, eds. *New Chicago Architecture: Beyond the International Style.* New York: Rizzoli, 1981.

Chappell, Sally A. Kitt. *Architecture and Planning of Graham, Anderson, Probst and White, 1912–1936.* Chicago: University of Chicago Press, 1992.

Chicago Architectural Journal.

Chicago Chapter, American Institute of Architects. *AIA Guide to Chicago Architecture.* New York: Harper & Row, 1993.

————. *Architecture Chicago.*

Cohen, Stuart E. *Chicago Architects: Documenting the Exhibition of the Same Name Organized by Laurence Booth, Stuart E. Cohen, Stanley Tigerman, and Benjamin Weese.* Chicago: Swallow Press, 1976.

Condit, Carl W. *Chicago, 1910–29: Building, Planning, and Urban Technology.* Chicago: University of Chicago Press, 1973.

————. *Chicago, 1930–70: Building, Planning, and Urban Technology.* Chicago: University of Chicago Press, 1974.

————. *The Chicago School of Architecture: A History of Commercial and Public*

Building in the Chicago Area, 1875–1925. Chicago: University of Chicago Press, 1964.

Connors, Joseph. *The Robie House of Frank Lloyd Wright.* Chicago: University of Chicago Press, 1984.

Conzen, Michael, Douglas Knox, and Dennis Cremin. *1848: Turning Point for Chicago, Turning Point for the Region.* Chicago: Newberry Library, 1998.

Cronon, William. *Nature's Metropolis: Chicago and the Great West.* New York: W. W. Norton, 1991.

Cummings, Kathleen Roy. *Architectural Records in Chicago: A Guide to Architectural Resources in Cook County and Vicinity.* Chicago: Art Institute of Chicago, 1981.

Darling, Sharon. *Chicago Furniture: Art, Craft, and Industry, 1833–1983.* New York: W. W. Norton, 1984.

De Wit, Wim, ed. *Louis Sullivan: The Function of Ornament.* New York: W. W. Norton, 1986.

Drury, John. *Old Chicago Houses.* 1945. Reprint, Chicago: University of Chicago Press, 1975.

Duis, Perry. *Chicago: Creating New Traditions.* Chicago: Chicago Historical Society, 1976.

Eaton, Leonard K. *Two Chicago Architects and Their Clients: Frank Lloyd Wright and Howard Van Doren Shaw.* Cambridge: MIT Press, 1969.

Einhorn, Robin L. *Property Rules: Political Economy in Chicago, 1833–1872.* Chicago: University of Chicago Press, 1991.

Fields, Jeanette S., ed. *A Guidebook to the Architecture of River Forest.* River Forest, Ill.: Architectural Guidebook Committee, River Forest Community Center, 1981.

Frederick Law Olmsted Society. *Riverside: A Village in a Park.* Riverside, Ill.: Frederick Law Olmsted Society, 1970.

Frueh, Erne R., and Florence Frueh. *The Second Presbyterian Church of Chicago: Art and Architecture.* Chicago: Second Presbyterian Church, 1978.

Gapp, Paul. *Paul Gapp's Chicago.* Chicago: Chicago Tribune, 1980.

Garner, John S., ed. *The Midwest in American Architecture.* Urbana: University of Illinois Press, 1991.

Giedion, Sigfried. *Mechanization Takes Command.* New York: Norton, 1948.

———. *Space, Time and Architecture: The Growth of a New Tradition.* Cambridge: Harvard University Press, 1954.

Gilbert, James. *Perfect Cities: Chicago's Utopias of 1893.* Chicago: University of Chicago Press, 1993.

Gray, Mary Lackritz. *A Guide to Chicago's Murals.* Chicago: University of Chicago Press, 2001.

Grube, Oswald W., Peter C. Pran, and Franz Schulze. *100 Years of Architecture in Chicago: Continuity of Structure and Form.* Chicago: J. Philip O'Hara, 1976.

Hales, Peter. *Constructing the Fair.* Chicago: Art Institute of Chicago, 1993.

Harrington, Elaine. *The Frank Lloyd Wright Home and Studio*. Stuttgart: Menges, 1996.

———. *Henry Hobson Richardson: JJ Glessner House, Chicago*. Tübingen: Wasmuth, 1993.

Hines, Thomas S. *Burnham of Chicago: Architect and Planner.* New York: Oxford University Press, 1974.

Hirsch, Arnold. *Making the Second Ghetto: Race and Housing in Chicago, 1940–1960.* Cambridge: Cambridge University Press, 1983.

Hoffman, Donald. *The Architecture of John Wellborn Root.* Baltimore: Johns Hopkins University Press, 1973.

———. *Frank Lloyd Wright's Robie House: The Illustrated Story of an Architectural Masterpiece.* New York: Dover, 1984.

———. *Understanding Frank Lloyd Wright's Architecture*. New York: Dover, 1995.

Johnson, Elmer W. *Chicago Metropolis 2020*. Chicago: University of Chicago Press, 2001.

Kamin, Blair. *Why Architecture Matters*. Chicago: University of Chicago Press, 2001.

Keating, Ann Durkin. *Building Chicago: Suburban Developers and the Creation of a Divided Metropolis.* Columbus: Ohio State University Press, 1988.

Lake Forest Foundation for Historic Preservation. *A Preservation Guide to National Register Properties, Lake Forest, Illinois.* Lake Forest, 1991.

Lambert, Phyllis, ed. *Mies in America*. New York: Abrams, 2001.

Lane, George. *Chicago Churches and Synagogues: An Architectural Pilgrimage.* Chicago: Loyola University Press, 1981.

Larson, Erik. *The Devil and the White City: Murder, Magic, and Madness at the Fair that Changed America*. New York: Crown, 2003.

Levine, Neil. *The Architecture of Frank Lloyd Wright*. Chicago: University of Chicago Press, 1998.

Lowe, David. *Lost Chicago.* 1978. 2nd ed. Boston: Houghton Mifflin, 2000.

Manny, Carter H., Jr. *Madlener House: Tradition and Innovation in Architecture.* Chicago: Graham Foundation, 1988.

Manson, Grant Carpenter. *Frank Lloyd Wright to 1910: The First Golden Age.* New York: Van Nostrand Reinhold, 1958.

Mayer, Harold M., and Richard C. Wade. *Chicago: Growth of a Metropolis.* Chicago: University of Chicago Press, 1969.

Menocal, Narciso. *Keck and Keck: Architects.* Madison, Wis.: Elvehjem Museum of Art, 1980.

Miller, Donald. *City of the Century: The Epic of Chicago and the Making of America*. New York: Simon & Schuster, 1996.

Miller, Ross. *American Apocalypse: The Great Fire and the Myth of Chicago.* Chicago: University of Chicago Press, 1990.

————. *Here's the Deal: The Buying and Selling of a Great American City*. New York: Alfred A. Knopf, 1996.

Molloy, Mary Alice. *Chicago since the Sears Tower: A Guide to New Downtown Buildings.* Chicago: Inland Architect Press, 1990.

O'Gorman, James F. *Three American Architects: Richardson, Sullivan, and Wright, 1865–1915.* Chicago: University of Chicago Press, 1991.

Pfeiffer, Bruce Brooks, ed. *Frank Lloyd Wright: Collected Writings.* 2 vols. New York: Rizzoli, 1992.

Pommer, Richard, David Spaeth, and Kevin Harrington. *In the Shadow of Mies: Ludwig Hilberseimer—Architect, Educator, and Urban Planner*. Chicago: Art Institute of Chicago, 1988.

Randall, Frank A. *History of the Development of Building Construction in Chicago.* 2nd ed., revised and expanded by John D. Randall. Urbana: University of Illinois Press, 1999.

Riley, Terence, ed. *Frank Lloyd Wright: Architect.* New York: Abrams, 1994.

Rowe, Colin. *The Mathematics of the Ideal Villa and Other Essays*. Cambridge: MIT Press, 1976.

Rydell, Robert. *All the World's a Fair*. Chicago: University of Chicago Press, 1984.

Saliga, Pauline, ed. *The Sky's the Limit: A Century of Chicago Skyscrapers.* New York: Rizzoli, 1990.

Salny, Stephen. *The Country Houses of David Adler*. New York: Norton, 2001.

Sanderson, Arlene, ed. *Wright Sites.* 3rd ed., revised. New York: Princeton Architectural Press, 2001.

Sawlisak, Karen. *Smoldering City: Chicagoans and the Great Fire, 1871–1874.* Chicago: University of Chicago Press, 1995.

Schulze, Franz. *The Farnsworth House*. Chicago: Lohan Associates, 1997.

————. *Mies van der Rohe: A Critical Biography.* Chicago: University of Chicago Press, 1985.

Schulze, Franz, and George E. Danforth, eds. *An Illustrated Catalog of the Mies van der Rohe Drawings in the Museum of Modern Art.* Part II, in 14 vols. New York: Garland, 1993.

Siry, Joseph M. *Carson Pirie Scott: Louis Sullivan and the Chicago Department Store.* Chicago: University of Chicago Press, 1988.

————. *The Chicago Auditorium Building: Adler and Sullivan's Architecture and the City*. Chicago: University of Chicago Press, 2002.

————. *Unity Temple: Frank Lloyd Wright and Architecture for Liberal Religion*. New York: Cambridge University Press, 1996.

Slaton, Deborah, ed. *Wild Onions: A Brief Guide to Landmarks and Lesser-Known Structures in Chicago's Loop.* Chicago: Association for Preservation Technology, 1989.

Smith, Carl S. *Chicago and the American Literary Imagination, 1880–1920.* Chicago: University of Chicago Press, 1984.

Sorell, Victor. *Guide to Chicago Murals, Yesterday and Today.* Chicago: Council on Fine Arts, 1979.

Sprague, Paul E. *Guide to Frank Lloyd Wright and Prairie School Architecture in Oak Park.* 2nd ed. Oak Park, Ill.: Village of Oak Park, 1978.

Stamper, John W. *Chicago's North Michigan Avenue: Planning and Development, 1900–1930.* Chicago: University of Chicago Press, 1991.

Storrer, William Allin. *The Architecture of Frank Lloyd Wright: A Complete Catalog.* 3rd ed. Chicago: University of Chicago Press, 2002.

———. *Frank Lloyd Wright Companion.* Chicago: University of Chicago Press, 1993.

Sullivan, Louis H. *The Autobiography of an Idea.* 1924. Reprint, New York: Dover Publications, 1956.

Suttles, Gerald D. *The Man-Made City: The Land-Use Confidence Game in Chicago.* Chicago: University of Chicago Press, 1990.

Tallmadge, Thomas E. *Architecture in Old Chicago.* 1941. Reprint, Chicago: University of Chicago Press, 1975.

Thorne, Martha, ed. *David Adler, Architect: The Elements of Style.* Chicago and New Haven: Art Institute of Chicago and Yale University Press, 2002.

Twombly, Robert. *Frank Lloyd Wright: His Life and His Architecture.* New York: John Wiley & Sons, 1979.

———. *Louis Sullivan: His Life and Work.* Chicago: University of Chicago Press, 1987.

Van Zanten, David. *Sullivan's City.* New York: Norton, 2000.

Weimann, Jeanne. *The Fair Woman: the Story of the Woman's Building, World's Columbian Exposition, Chicago, 1893.* Chicago: Academy, 1981.

Wille, Lois. *Forever Open, Clear and Free: The Struggle for Chicago's Lakefront.* 2nd ed. Chicago: University of Chicago Press, 1991.

Wright, Frank Lloyd. *An Autobiography.* 3rd ed., rev. New York: Horizon Press, 1977.

Wright, Gwendolyn. *Moralism and the Model Home: Domestic Architecture and Cultural Conflict in Chicago, 1873–1913.* Chicago: University of Chicago Press, 1980.

Zukowsky, John, ed. *Chicago Architecture, 1872–1922: Birth of a Metropolis.* Munich: Prestel Verlag, 1987.

———. *Chicago Architecture and Design, 1923–1993: Reconfiguration of an American Metropolis.* Chicago and Munich: Art Institute of Chicago and Prestel Verlag, 1993.

Glossary

acroterion (pl. acroteria) The pedestal and the decorated form it supports capping the gable of a building.

Art Deco A decorative style widely employed in architecture of the 1930s and based upon traditional forms stylized and slightly abstracted. Angular, zigzag, and geometric shapes are characteristic. The name is derived from the Paris Exposition International des Arts Decoratifs et Industrielles Moderne of 1925. Also known as Style Moderne.

balloon frame A system of wooden framing in which bearing walls are made of studs rising the full height of the frame and attached to floor joists by nails. Commercial availability of such components in the early nineteenth century enabled semi-skilled laborers to erect a house more quickly than ever before, thus hastening the settlement of the American West.

balustrade A system of railings on the edge of a porch, balcony, roof deck, or staircase.

baroque A style of architecture and ornamentation begun in seventeenth-century Italy and based upon Renaissance forms that have been heavily embellished.

The name implies a quality of grandiosity deriving from the use of color and often of curvilinear and sculptural masses.

bay A regularly repeated space in the vertical composition of the outer wall of a building.

cantilevered Built with horizontal beams supported at only one end and made of material strong enough to resist collapse at the other end.

capital The element at the top of a column or of any other vertical support in a building.

cartouche An elaborate ornamental frame, often marked by highly embellished carving.

chamfer The beveled or rounded edge where two surfaces meet in an exterior or interior angle.

Chicago frame The transformation of the fact of the gridded, three-dimensional Cartesian frame of tall buildings into a metaphor of modernism, technology, and efficiency.

Chicago school Architects known for their interest in developing a frankly modern architecture, free of subservience to the past, in which the metal frame provided a source of order in large commercial buildings and the wooden balloon frame a source of freedom in suburban houses.

Chicago window A window occupying the full width of the bay and divided into a large fixed sash flanked by a narrow movable sash at each side.

colonnette A small column, often used decoratively rather than functionally for support.

Corinthian In classical architecture, the slenderest and most elaborate of the three ancient Greek orders, readily recognizable for tall capitals decorated with ornate effigies of acanthus leaves.

cornice The projecting horizontal member at the top of a wall; often a decorative development of the eaves of the roof.

Cor-ten steel A material process by which the natural oxidation of steel (rust) becomes the protective surface of the material.

cruciform Cross-shaped, usually referring to a building plan.

cupola A terminal structure, rising above a main roof.

curtain wall A nonsupportive outer wall of a building, usually consisting of a lightweight material, like glass.

dentils A series of blocklike projections forming a molding, borrowed from the Greek Ionic order.

Doric In classical architecture, one of the three ancient Greek orders. It is notable for a sturdiness and simplicity of form, most evident in the thickness of the column and a capital that features a square, cushionlike block. The Doric frieze consists of two alternating decorative elements, the triglyph and the metope.

entablature In classical architecture, the horizontal element resting on the columns and made up of architrave, frieze, and cornice.

facade The face or front of a building.

fanlight A semi-circular or semi-elliptical window over a door, usually with radiating bars like the ribs of a fan.

festoon A decorative garland, sculptured in relief as a loop between two points.

flamboyant Gothic Flamelike, usually curving, tongues of wooden or masonry tracery, often in large openings.

gable The upper part of a terminal wall, under the ridge of a pitched roof.

Georgian The architectural style developed during the reigns of Queen Anne and the four Georges, 1702–1830.

Gothic The architecture of the thirteenth, fourteenth, and fifteenth centuries, characterized by the use of pointed arches, buttresses, rib vaulting, and stone tracery.

Guastavino-vaulted Beginning in 1880, the Spanish-born Rafael Guastavino developed a number of innovative tile-vaulting techniques, derived from the Catalan masonry tradition. His son introduced them to the United States in 1881.

Ionic One of the ancient classical orders, most distinctive for the twin, opposed, helical volutes of the capitals.

lintel A horizontal span between two upright elements, or over a window.

Mannerist Referring to the elaborate, highly stylized manner affected by the artists and architects of sixteenth-century Italy.

masonry Construction using plaster, concrete, and the application of stone, brick, tile, etc., sometimes with mortar.

molding An element of construction or decoration that introduces a variety of outlines or profiles on the edge or surface of a wall.

mullion An upright division member between a series of windows or doors.

narthex The enclosed, often covered, space in a Christian church, prior to entering the nave.

nave The main portion of a church or cathedral occupied by the worshipers (excluding the transepts).

oriel A projecting window supported on brackets or corbels.

ornament Detail applied to plain surfaces of a building, whether by sculpture, incising, painting, or any other method, for the purpose of embellishment.

Palladian windows An opening characterized by three parts, the center one having a semicircular top and the two flanking openings having flat tops that are in the same line as the springing point of the center curve.

parapet A low retaining wall at the edge of a roof, porch, or terrace.

pier Any upright structure used as a principal support by itself or as part of a wall.

pilaster An engaged pier of shallow depth.

pile A column driven into the ground as part of a foundation.

portico An entrance porch.

Prairie school The work of architects based on the ideas and example of Louis H. Sullivan and Frank Lloyd Wright, especially an architectural equivalent to the horizontality of the prairie.

Romanesque (or Norman) The architecture of Europe ranging in various regional types from about 800 through the twelfth century. It is marked by heavy walls and round arches.

sanctuary In a Christian church, the area around the main altar.

setback The device in buildings where the wall plane is seen to recede in a regular and progressive manner. Especially associated with the Art Deco.

shear-wall core An element of a tall building designed to take the load of the wind. Many modern buildings have isolated the shear wall at the center of the structure, usually incorporating the elevator banks, thus permitting column-free spaces between the core and the curtain wall, which transfers wind loads to the shear-wall core.

spandrel Originally the three-sided web of material on either side of an arch; over time and by extension, it has been applied to the horizontal panels in the curtain walls of concrete or metal-framed buildings.

spire A tall tower roof, tapering up to a point.

stringcourse A continuous horizontal band, plain or molded, on an exterior wall.

stucco Plaster for exterior walls.

terra-cotta Cast and fired clay bricks, usually larger and more intricately modeled than bricks.

transept Either of the side spaces perpendicular to the nave and usually separated from it by columns, in a church of cruciform plan.

trumps A form, usually curved, projecting from the plane of the wall of a building well above the ground. Early uses were often stairs, later uses are often a stacked series of projecting bays.

truss A structure made up of a network of members, often in triangular arrangements so as to provide a rigid framework.

vaulted Roofed by arched masonry, or having the appearance of a roof of arched masonry.

Credits

The images are organized according to the order of their appearance in the book, and by entry number, not by page number. Some of the photographs in this book illustrate buildings in earlier stages. This was done intentionally, to provide images that reflect the designers' original motives.

Frontispiece Chicago Theater, 1927. Photograph by Kaufman and Fabry, courtesy of Chicago Historical Society (ICHi-10987)

Preface Auditorium Theatre, interior. Photograph by Leslie Schwartz

Introduction Aerial view of Michigan Avenue cliff. Photograph © Mark Segal

The Commercial Core Daley Plaza. Photograph by Leslie Schwartz

Michigan Avenue Cliff Facades on South Michigan Avenue. Photograph by Leslie Schwartz

1. Congress Hotel. Photograph by Daniel Wilson
2. Auditorium Building. Photograph by J. W. Taylor, courtesy of The Art Institute of Chicago, Architecture Photography Collection
3. Fine Arts Building. Photograph by Barbara Crane

Index